Marriage Dreams Do Come True

Experiencing God's Version of Happily Ever After

Shaun and Amy Gustafson

Marriage Dreams Do Come True
Experiencing God's Version of Happily Ever After
by Shaun and Amy Gustafson

Printed in the United States of America

ISBN 9781615794911

www.xulonpress.com

CONTENTS

v

DEDICATION

We dedicate this book to our parents for the years of love they have poured into our lives.

To Shaun's father, Stan Gustafson, who instilled into us excellent people skills and genuine compassion for people and who dedicated Shaun to the Lord as a brand new baby for the call of ministry;

To Shaun's mother, Judy Gustafson, who is now with the Lord, for being a beautiful example of daily seeking God and having a relationship with Him, leaving us a legacy to follow;

To Amy's father, Don Cooper, who taught us strength, diligence, and a never-give-up attitude and has always been there to show support;

To Amy's mother, Dawn Cooper, who has continually inspired us with her words, believed in and supported the call of God on our life in any and every way she could think of, and taught us to sincerely love and praise others;

To our mother-in-love, Stan's new wife, Nancy Gustafson, your generous, kind heart and sincere love for people are an answer to prayer for our family. Thank you for treating us like your own;

Between all of our parents, we know there are literally thousands of hours of prayers that have gone into our life and ministry. We honor you for all you have done and continue to be to us. Thank you.

ACKNOWLEDGEMENTS

We give praise and thanks to God for His love, goodness, and inspiration in writing this book. His love for marriage is amazing.

A special thank you to those who have so graciously helped us with the writing of this book through insights, creative ideas, and manuscript reading:

James and Catherine Tito
Terry and Jana Meskill
Jim and Carleen Higgins
Greg and Heather Main
Melody Dornink
Rita Kramer Joerg

Last, but not least, thank you to all of our family members. We appreciate you.

FOREWORD

I want to commend my dear friends, Shaun and Amy, for this masterful, practical, heartfelt, and anointed marriage masterpiece. This book can easily be used by any minister or college professor as a textbook on Biblical marriage.

It is clear this is not a work of man, but of the Holy Spirit of the living God. It will show you that it is not what we are, or what we possess in ourselves that God is depending on, but what He can make of us when we obey His Word.

As you read this most inspiring book, you will be introduced to many dynamic marriage principles that will empower you and your mate to conform to the image of Christ in your marriage relationship.

If you take time to pause and meditate on the Scriptures shared, there is no doubt that you and your mate will live together blessed with joy, peace, and happiness for many years to come.

This work is destined to be a success.

Wendell Hope, Sr.
Executive Director/Pastor
Tulsa Dream Center
Tulsa, OK

Introduction

One of the most powerful forces any relationship in life has going for it, is the force of commitment. Your pursuit of marriage teaching is a reflection of a committed heart. We applaud you for your commitment! We trust you will become more effective in your marriage, family, and relationships through the teaching in this book.

Whether you are married, engaged, or have a dream to be married one day, this book shares easy-to-apply principles which lead to a successful future. We started searching the Bible to find the truth about what our part is in having the marriage of our dreams. We knew that if we could learn and apply what God taught, marriage success would be inevitable.

God's heart is to build successful marriages and families in church, business, and community leaders. God has made it possible for people to achieve lasting success both at home and in your career. We once heard one of the wealthiest businessmen in the world say that God put it in his heart to get his home life in order, and that if he did, he would achieve lasting success in business.

As Proverbs 19:8 says, *"He who gets wisdom loves his own soul; he who keeps understanding will find good."* This is our prayer for you as you read what is before you. We pray each chapter will help you gain greater understanding and wisdom for experiencing the marriage of your dreams and lasting improvements in your home.

We believe you will see and understand, at greater levels than ever before, the plan and purpose God has for your marriage and family. You and your family are called and destined by God to achieve greatness. We are confident that what you are about to read is going to greatly help you achieve your God-given purpose in life.

God believes in you and so do we!

Pastors Shaun and Amy

Chapter 1

Right Thinking

**...And if *there is* any virtue and if *there is*
anything praiseworthy—meditate on these things
(Philippians 4:8).**

AMY: UNCONDITIONAL LOVE

I remember as clearly as if it were yesterday, my first big example of Shaun's unconditional love. I had spoken something to Shaun and then continued on with what I was doing. Within a few minutes, I felt convicted in my heart, realizing what I had just said and the tone of voice I used was disrespectful. I went into our living room where Shaun was sitting to apologize. I said to him, "What are you thinking about?" He responded, "I'm thinking about all of the reasons you are such a wonderful wife and why I love being married to you!" I was astounded and even more convicted. "Why would you be thinking about that? I was coming to apologize for what I said to you a few minutes ago." With a smile he said, "The call of God on our life is too important for me to allow offense into my heart, so instead of letting myself have hurt feelings, I countered it with good thoughts. Even if you had not apologized I wouldn't have minded because I know your heart and you normally are very kind with your words."

I once heard someone say we tend to judge others by their actions; however, we judge ourselves by our intentions. Shaun's example changed my life forever because he did the opposite of what many people would naturally want to do. He disciplined his flesh and walked in love, even when I wasn't. He did not allow himself to behave rudely, to be provoked, nor to think evil. I always remember his example when I have opportunity to get offended. I remind myself that meditating on a wrong someone did or said towards me is a response I cannot participate in if I want to walk in the goodness God has planned for my life.

SHAUN AND AMY: THINKING ON THE RIGHT THINGS

When Paul wrote his letter to the Christians in Philippi, he encouraged them to *choose* to have Christ-like thoughts, stating,

Finally, brethren, whatever things are true, whatever things *are* noble, whatever things *are* just, whatever things *are* pure, whatever things *are* lovely, whatever things *are* of good report, if *there is* any virtue and if *there is* anything praise- worthy—meditate on these things. The things which you learned and received and heard and saw in me, these do, and the God of peace will be with you (Philippians 4:8-9).

Paul understood the power in our thought-life. He knew when we meditate on good things, God's peace is then estab- lished in our hearts and in our homes. This truth applies to every area of our lives, but let us take a closer look at its impact on marriage.

Most of us do not have any problem thinking good of our spouse when he or she is kind to us and doing the things we like them to do. The question to ask is—do we put this Scripture into operation in our lives when our spouse has not invested time with us or has not met our needs?

Notice Paul *did not say*, "Finally brethren, whatever things are a lie of the devil, whatever things are unkind, what- ever things are unloving, whatever things are an evil report, if there is any immorality and anything worth condemning— meditate on these things." No, Paul knew that these things are what a person naturally wants to do, so he purposefully instructed the church to meditate on the good because he knew that it would have to be an intentional effort on our part!

SHAUN: DRAWING OUT THE BEST IN OTHERS

Whatever we meditate on about others, good or bad, we will draw out more of that in their personality. You have heard the statement, "That person really knows how to bring out the best in me." If we truly believe in someone, it will be demonstrated through our actions, words, and even prayers for the person.

When I was in Bible college, there was a young man in his early twenties in one of my classes who was asked by the professor to share his testimony with the class. His birth mother had been a drug addict who brought him, only a few days old, into a business and left him with the people at the desk, saying she could not take care of the baby. A loving Christian family who had been praying for a baby boy quickly adopted him.

His new mother brought him to the doctor and was told he had so much cocaine in his body that he would certainly be a drug addict himself by the age of nine or ten. The mom was also told he would never be intelligent, he would have various abnormalities, and he would be little and frail with a weak immune system throughout life. The parents refused to believe the doctor's report.

His mom prayed over him daily and believed for God to make him strong and intelligent and that he would become a mighty vessel for God. She prayed the blood of Jesus shed on the cross would cleanse his system and cancel every adverse effect of the drugs he had in the womb. As he grew, they saw all of the prayers answered. He became a strong, healthy, tall, and very intelligent young man with a wonderful gift for preaching.

His testimony then became even more amazing. When he was a young teen, his dad walked away from God and divorced his mother for another woman. He felt bitter, yet each day at their meals together he would hear his mom pray with a heart of love and compassion, believing God to somehow draw his dad back to Jesus. His mother's example of unconditional love and forgiveness amazed him and eventually opened his heart to have compassion for his father.

One day, after a few years had passed, he received a visit from his father. His dad apologized for what he had done. He had asked God to forgive him and had come to ask his son for his forgiveness as well. My classmate forgave his dad, and they were reconciled in their relationship. The next day his dad died of a heart attack.

Certainly it was not God's will for the father to die prematurely. John 10:10 tells us it is the devil that comes to steal, kill, and destroy. Thankfully, however, he did repent before passing on. This young man's mother drew the best from her son through her example of unconditional love and also helped draw her husband back to the Lord through prayers of faith.

As it states in Luke 6:45, whatever is in our heart in abundance will come out. This young man's mother chose to have a pure heart of forgiveness with the help of God even after her husband abandoned her and their child. She meditated on the Word rather than dwelling on the negative. She always had love and forgiveness coming out of her mouth and her son only heard her speak kindness toward his father.

What a wonderful example this man's mother is to us as believers. When we make every effort to fill our mind and heart with good thoughts based on the Word, then the love of God will always come out when we speak. No matter what our situation, there will be an abundance of His love in our hearts.

AMY: EATING THE FRUIT OF OUR LIPS

Why is it important to consistently speak the right things? It is important for the same reason farmers do not want weeds growing with the crops they plant in their fields. I remember growing up on a farm. We would go into the field and pick weeds when the crop was in the growth stages because my dad did not want the weeds to choke out the soybeans. He wanted a great harvest, so we worked to get rid of the weeds. Then as the sun shone and the rain watered the plants, they grew beautifully, and a bountiful harvest was attained when the soybeans were picked.

Likewise, our words are also seeds that will produce a harvest. As Proverbs 13:2 states, *"A man shall eat well by the fruit of his mouth..."* Whatever we are reaping right now is a result of what we have been sowing in our past. Therefore, from this moment on, if we want a harvest of excellent fruit in our life, our marriage, and our children's behavior, it is important that we consistently speak the right words over each of these areas.

When we speak the promises of God rather than verbalizing what may be taking place in the natural, we will eventually begin to see a change. Is this always easy to do? No. Does this mean we deny reality? No. This means we stop meditating on and repeatedly speaking the problems and rather begin to speak God's promises and God's ability in our situation. Whatever we magnify will become a giant in our life.

The choice God wants us to make, regarding consistently speaking loving words and God's promises about a person or situation, is addressed in James 3:9-12. James speaks of the importance of taming our tongues by saying,

With it we bless our God and Father, and with it we curse men, who have been made in the similitude of God. Out of the same mouth proceed blessing and cursing. My brethren these things ought not

to be so. Does a spring send forth fresh water and bitter from the same opening? Can a fig tree, my brethren, bear olives, or a grapevine bear figs? Thus no spring yields both salt water and fresh.

James said when someone blesses God with his or her mouth, then speaks unkind things about a man made in the image of God, it is not right. Just as a tree cannot produce fruit of a different kind than it was planted to be, so we can be confident the words we speak will produce fruit. If we speak kindness and compliments to our spouse and children, we will eventually see the fruit in their personalities because they will feel loved. If we train ourselves to speak life and blessing to others, and do not plant bad seeds by refusing to speak negative no matter how the person may act, we will eventually reap a good harvest.

SHAUN AND AMY: SPEAKING THE WORD OVER OUR SPOUSE

We used to lead a Bible study for married couples a number of years ago. One couple in the group was having large marital problems. Although the husband had accepted Christ years ago and attended church, he was not living his life according to the Word.

Our pastor called for a mandatory separation for the physical safety of the wife and kids when he found out the situation in the home. In addition, they started Christian marital counseling, the husband attended Christian based anger management classes, and another man in the church who was a mature believer became a mentor and accountability partner to the husband.

We will call the couple Jake and Sheila. Sometimes Sheila would come alone to our study, and sometimes they were together. After we did our teaching and study, we would provide the opportunity for discussion. Occasionally, when Jake was not there, Sheila would proceed to tell everyone in the group about their marital problems. She would share numerous stories from the prior week of how irresponsible, selfish, and unloving her husband had been, including everything from anger outbursts to his buying her flowers with bad checks.

One day the Lord dealt with us about Sheila and her repeatedly telling all their personal information and degrading her husband in front of everyone. The Lord clearly placed on our hearts the thought that, "She is eating the fruit of her lips." Her husband definitely needed help, but she was drawing even more negatives out in him because she would meditate on his behavior and repeat it to everyone who would listen. The more she told people about his poor behavior, the more he would increase in the negative actions.

After one Bible study we visited with her about this issue, giving her the Scriptures of Proverbs 12:14 and Proverbs 18:21, which remind us we will eat the fruit of our lips, good or bad. We encouraged her to share what she needed to with the pastor and those in leadership who were counseling them and also to feel free to ask us to pray for specific areas. However, we advised her to stop telling those around her the personal details about mistakes her husband made.

Instead we suggested she start picturing him through what the Bible says about him as a believer and looking for the good things he did do. We encouraged her to focus on and compliment every good thing she could find. She said she understood what we were saying and would apply it.

Several weeks later Sheila came and told us she had been doing as we had suggested, only sharing details with those who really needed to hear them. She had also started making an effort to think positive thoughts about her husband and compliment him. She said things were definitely improving. They continued with us for several months until the Bible study concluded.

I talked to her several years later and found out their relationship had continued to steadily improve and they were now happily married again. He had become a genuinely loving, responsible husband and father. She told me she was so thankful she had persevered through the many storms and not divorced him. It was hard on her and the children during that long period of time, but if she hadn't stayed with it, her kids would not have seen how powerful God is. He was able to change their dad, and that was an absolute miracle.

SEEING OUR SPOUSE AS A NEW CREATION

2 Corinthians 5:17 states, *"Therefore, if anyone is in Christ, he is a new creation; old things have passed away; behold, all things have become new."* Sometimes if we or someone close to us is still hanging onto old things that Jesus has redeemed us from, we may need to start picturing ourselves or that person for who God created them to be, rather than who they are currently acting like.

We can pray Scripture over them, knowing that God can and will transform our loved ones through His Word. If you have never used Scripture to pray for someone, simply take a verse and put their name in it, then use it as a prayer for their life. For example,

> *Father, I pray that Christ would dwell in (name's) heart through faith; that he or she, being rooted and grounded in love, may be able to comprehend with all the saints what is the width and length and depth and height – to know the love of Christ which passes knowledge; that (name) may be filled with all of Your fullness God (taken from Ephesians 3:17-19).*

As we read this Scripture, we can picture our husband or wife in the Scripture. By faith, we believe God is working on their heart and they are learning to walk in love toward others. We can thank God that our loved one's life is being transformed by His love because God is truth and therefore His word is truth (see John 7:28, 14:6, 16:11, 1 John 5:20). The power of life is in our tongue as we speak His Word over our spouse, our family, and ourselves.

Another great Scripture to pray is 1 Corinthians 13:4-8. Put your name and then your spouse's name in it as you read and picture yourself and your spouse acting this way, because through Christ we are able to consistently be Christlike in our actions. If your spouse is not yet committed to God, take Romans 10:9-10 and pray,

I thank you God that (spouse's name) now confesses with (his or her) mouth the Lord Jesus and believes in (his or her) heart that You raised Jesus from the dead, and (he or she) is now saved. For with (his or her) heart (he or she) has now believed onto righteousness, and with (his or her) mouth (he or she) has now made confession unto salvation.

Romans 4:17 shows us God calls those things that be not as though they were. As we pray Scripture over those we love, we are applying God's Word to bring His life-changing power into the situation. As we are faithful to pray Scripture daily over our spouse and meditate on praiseworthy reports rather than focusing on the negative, we will see significant results because God's Word does not return void (see Isaiah 55:11).

LOVE NEVER FAILS

We know a certain woman who became a Christian, committing her life to the Lord after she and her husband married. Although her husband wanted nothing to do with God or church, she was always compassionate toward him. Her greatest desire was to see him receive God's free love and forgiveness through Jesus.

We were amazed when we visited with her. She never once spoke unkind words about him even though he was often inconsiderate toward her. She always got tears in her eyes and said, "All I want is to know that one day, when he dies, he will go to heaven and not hell."

She focused on the best in him continually and would never complain about him or their marriage. She also invested time each day praying for other marriages where the wife went to church but the husband did not. It wasn't long before he asked Jesus into his heart and now has a close relationship with God himself!

This wife is a great example of how we are able to choose our own thoughts and words; our circumstances do not have to dictate them. When we make a conscious choice to forget the past and not meditate on wrongs done to us, we are then able to focus on and speak the promises of God over our life and the lives of those around us. When we do these two things—meditate on praiseworthy reports and pray God's

Word—we are truly able to reach forward to the good things God has in store for us. As Paul said,

> **Brethren, I do not count myself to have apprehended; but one thing I do, forgetting those things which are behind and reaching forward to those things which are ahead, I press toward the goal for the prize of the upward call of God in Christ Jesus (Philippians 3:13-14).**

You may be asking yourself, "Is it really possible to forget bad things that have happened to me?" According to Matthew 19:26, *"...With God all things are possible."* When we study Scripture, we find the key to forgetting wrongs done to us is love. Love is a choice, rather than merely a feeling. We let go of past hurts by choice, and God's love will help us do this. Let us look again at Ephesians 3:14-19:

> **For this reason I bow my knees to the Father of our Lord Jesus Christ, from whom the whole family in heaven and earth is named, that He would grant to you, according to the riches of His glory, to be strengthened with might through His Spirit in the inner man, that Christ may dwell in your hearts through faith; that you, being rooted and grounded in love, may be able to comprehend with all the saints what is the width and length**

**and depth and height—to know the love of Christ
which passes knowledge; that you may be filled
with all the fullness of God.**

Often when people read this passage, they assume the
"saint" mentioned above is simply making reference to a
godly person here on earth, but it is not. The Hebrew word
for that kind of saint is used in Psalm 116:15 which states,
"Precious in the sight of the Lord is the death of His saints."
The word used for "saints" in this Psalm means "godly man,
good, holy (one), merciful" (Strong's #2623).

In Ephesians 3 the word translated as "saints" specifically refers to "God, an angel, a saint, a sanctuary" (Strong's
#6918). This means Paul is praying for believers to be
grounded in and understand all forms of God's love just like
God, His angels, and the saints who already live with Him
in heaven!

You may be wondering, "What does understanding God's
love like those who already live with Him in heaven have to
do with not meditating on wrongs someone has done to me?"
Everything and we will illustrate why.

When Shaun was having time with the Lord, preparing
to preach the message for his mother's memorial service,
it was clearly placed on his heart that one of the things he
was supposed to tell people was to think about the good
things they had done for his mom during her life here on

earth, rather than thinking of any regrets. Shaun realized this thought was very scriptural.

Colossians 3:2 encourages us, *"Set your mind on things above, not on things on the earth."* Everything in heaven is good and lovely because God is the focus of heaven and He is good and loving. People in heaven certainly think only of the good and loving memories from earth now that they are with Him, therefore we also can choose to be heavenly minded and only look for the good in people. We are able to do this more and more as we *"know the love of Christ which passes knowledge"* (Ephesians 3:19).

In the presence of God, who is love, there is no desire to meditate on hurts from the past or flaws in a person's character. Even when Jesus hung on the cross He said, *"Father, forgive them, for they do not know what they do"* (Luke 23:34). When a person truly experiences God's unconditional love in their life, they passionately desire to show God's love to those around them so others can experience His goodness also.

It has been said that if you choose to remain in your pain, you will stay the same. We would like to add, "If you choose to meditate on what is right, you will be a vessel through which God can shine His light!" *Anyone can find imperfections in people. The real skill is choosing to look past mistakes and focus on the good in others.*

When we bestow honor and admiration on those around us consistently, particularly on our spouse and children, we will receive the benefit of a peaceful loving home. Our prayer for you is that you will daily choose to be a vessel of light for God, ministering His love to those in your home and to those you encounter in this world.

Keys to Thinking the Right Things Toward Your Spouse

1. Daily look for things to praise.

2. Focus on the positive.

3. Refuse to speak negative about your spouse.

4. Speak the promises of God over your spouse.

5. Think of your spouse as a precious child of God.

Chapter 2

Pray Together – Stay Together

**Again I say to you that if two of you agree on
earth concerning anything that they ask, it
will be done for them by My Father in heaven
(Matthew 18:19).**

"We deeply love each other and know it was God
who brought us together. We just don't understand why we fight so much. On a regular basis one of us
gets upset or irritated with the other about something."

Ben and Shelly verbalized thoughts experienced by
many couples. Through further discussions we found they
were both raised in broken families. Ben had never met his
father nor had any male role model in the home. Shelly had
some role models, but was raised in a separated family much
of her life.

Unfortunately, this is very common in the day we live.
Many people have grown up with either poor examples or

no examples of the skills and unconditional love required to make marriage last a lifetime. Within a short time, they begin to follow the behavior patterns they observed in their parents marriage or just make an attempt based on what makes them feel loved. They enter marriage hoping to receive unconditional love, but having little to no idea how to give unconditional love.

Ben and Shelly longed for the peace and joy God intended for marriage and asked us if we would impart any truths we had discovered. We visited together, sharing the main key to unity God had taught us. God had shown us through His Word that if we would pray together for a time each day, we would have peace, unity, and single-mindedness in our marriage relationship all day long.

This is shown in Acts 4:24, which states the group of believers gathered together and *"...raised their voice to God with one accord..."* Later, verses 31 and 32 continue with,

And when they had prayed, the place where they were assembled together was shaken; and they were all filled with the Holy Spirit, and they spoke the word of God with boldness. Now the multitude of those who believed were of one heart and one soul; neither did anyone say that any of the things he possessed was his own, but they had all things in common.

Did you notice the three key effects unified prayer caused among the believers in this passage of Scripture? First, when the believers prayed together they increased in boldness of sharing the Word. God desires for us to be a witness to unbelievers as well as to other Christians around us. This is done verbally as well as through our being a living testimony of God's goodness. As you and your spouse pray together, you both increase in boldness about sharing and demonstrating the love and goodness of God with those around you.

Second, praying together resulted in them having one heart and one soul (unity), meaning no difference of opinion for direction, purpose or motives. James 1:7 tells us a double-minded man is unstable in all his ways. A marriage with two people trying to go their own direction, rather than God's unified direction, is also unstable. However, as you and your spouse pray together, double-mindedness will leave your marriage and single-mindedness will enter to unify the two of you as one heart and one soul.

Third, the believers' unified prayer resulted in selflessness rather than selfishness. The last passage says they did not count their possessions as their own but shared with whoever had need. Selfishness is a large problem in many marriages today; however, this Scripture shows us how to overcome this destructive behavior and become a loving, sharing spouse. When we as a married couple pray together, we are putting Christ at the center of our relationship. God is then able to do a work in us to encourage a sharing and giving spirit, which will produce a "what's mine is yours" attitude. This is the way God intended marriage to be.

After we explained all of these benefits to Ben and Shelly, Ben shared that he questioned whether this would truly help their relationship. "Let's do this," we said. "You said you have disagreements almost everyday. Try praying together at least 15 minutes every morning for just one week. Then come back and tell us the results." We also added, "One more thing, make sure you do your prayer together first thing, before you engage in conversation with each other, otherwise you may get in a disagreement first and end up not praying at all."

One week later Ben and Shelly arrived for our meeting. Before they even said a word, we could tell things had improved. Their countenance had brightened, and their body language towards each other showed a new spark and tenderness. They excitedly shared with us that in only one week there had been dramatic changes. They both agreed the arguments had diminished by about 90 percent. With a smile Ben said, "The remaining 10 percent of disagreements happened only when we didn't start the day with prayer first."

Ben and Shelly had quickly learned and proven that God's Word will always work for us when we put it into practice. Isn't it good to know God didn't just throw a man and woman together with their opposite strengths, gifts, and abilities and say, "Boy, I don't know how they are ever going to get along with each other?" No, God made marriage to be a work of art, and He gave us a manual to follow on how to have strong relationships. He made man and woman's opposite characteristics to compliment and strengthen each other and to be a powerful force in the earth for His kingdom. He created marriage to be a gift, and it can be for you today.

No matter the current condition of your marriage, there is hope. Remember God said, *"Love never fails"* (1 Corinthians 13:8). We can take God at His Word and ask Him for help to love our spouse with His kind of love.

Let us say here that doing things God's way in marriage is not always easy. During the hard times, remember this great quote from Charles Kettering: "No one would have ever crossed the ocean if he could have gotten off the ship during a storm." This is also true with marriage. If we give up when things are the worst, we will never be able to experience God's best. A rainbow comes after the storm.

It is often in the early years that many couples face their biggest challenges. Studies show most divorces take place within the first seven years of a marriage. The wedding is joyous, but then the challenges of life in a sin-filled world show up and people have to daily make the choice, *"...as for me and my house we will serve the Lord"* (Joshua 24:15). Many couples happily married over thirty years tell us the toughest years were in the first ten, but they are thankful they worked it out. They would not have had all the joyous years together if they had not persevered and worked through those early challenges!

Studies have shown that couples who choose to stay together and work out their problems are reportedly happier than those who become divorced.[1] In order to achieve success in life and marriage, it is essential to learn how to overcome the rough waves. Through the challenging times, many couples begin to take their frustrations out on family and associate feelings from life's disappointments with their spouse or children. They may become disillusioned with their marriage, thinking the relationship is their main problem. However in reality, marriage and family was designed by God to be a haven from life's challenges.

When a couple puts God first and builds a spiritual bond with each other through daily prayer and going to church as a family, this is the first step in building a strong relationship that will weather the test of time. Then when tough times come, they have a strong foundation that is not easily shaken.

A couple can be so spiritually out of touch with God and each other that they do not even know this important bond is missing in their relationship. Then one day something major happens and they realize they have lost (or never developed) their spiritual foundation. Once a couple chooses to put God first and build or reestablish their spiritual bond, God is able to move mightily on their behalf. He can and will establish deeper love and excitement, as well as reveal His divine plan and purpose for their union together.

GOD'S PLAN FOR MARRIAGE

God's kind of marriage is like two masterfully trained and highly skilled tennis players who are experts at playing doubles together. Whenever a ball comes at them, they know instinctively how to work as a team to be the most effective. At times they get tired, yet they don't give up. They win the large majority of their matches because of their diligent practice together and their acquired skill, and the victory is exhilarating.

Likewise, because of living in an imperfect world, there are challenges we encounter. Yet, realizing we are on the same team and facing them together, we become much more effective, and the process is exceedingly more enjoyable and rewarding.

To be the best team possible, we could think of our daily prayer time together as our marriage unity practice. Just as a sports team practices together daily before they ever come to the big game day, so we must practice unity through prayer before trials and obstacles come in order to be consistently victorious. This time gets us started on the same page as a couple with a unified vision and unified thoughts. We are then able to experience increased marriage stability and emotional peace throughout the day.

We compare daily prayer to a welding torch. An experienced welder will tell you that when a truly good weld is made with two pieces of metal, it is stronger at the bond of the weld than at any other place on the metal.

This is what prayer does to a marriage. It welds it together so perfectly that when challenges occur, rather than having conflict and division, the marriage will not bend to the pressures. Both husband and wife continue to walk in love towards each other, refusing to allow strife in their relationship.

SHAUN: BUILDING UNITY

In Deuteronomy 30:32 we find that through the power of God on the Israelites' side, one person was able to chase a thousand, and with two people they put ten thousand to flight! We have a covenant right to the same favor the Israelites had and even greater through Jesus Christ our Lord. If we can have the ability to chase ten thousand rather than one thousand spiritually, why would we not take advantage of it?

The Bible also says when two or three agree concerning anything it shall be done (see Matthew 18:19-20). A married couple in unity is clearly two in agreement. There is no stronger union between humans than the marriage covenant because it represents our relationship with God. Therefore, the enemy tries to make married couples ignorant of their power in agreement together.

We experienced a large challenge in our early years of marriage. There were some inappropriate situations going on at my place of work. Amy and I had discussed that I should start looking for a new job. One day after a situation occurred, I resigned and had to go home to tell Amy I had left my job and we were going to have to move quickly because my work was connected to our housing.

As I walked in the door, I wasn't sure how to give Amy the news, so I just blurted it out, "I resigned from my job and we have to find a new place to live." To my surprise, Amy got a huge smile on her face and said, "Praise the Lord! It's about time! Let's praise the Lord right now for all the great things He is about to do on our behalf."

We praised the Lord with all of our hearts, thanking him for the new job I would soon have and the better home we knew by faith He had already prepared for us. Within one week we found a beautiful new home that was much more than what we had before. Within three weeks I had a new job that paid twice as much! The job also had insurance benefits, which we did not have before, and in addition to all this, they even gave reimbursement for my college tuition! During this situation as well as others, we never became angry at each other nor allowed bitterness to enter, because of our unity through daily prayer and trust that God would continue to keep us in his will.

SHAUN AND AMY: HOW TO PRAY TOGETHER

During our prayer time we give God praise for His goodness and we also let our requests be made known to the Lord with thanksgiving (see Philippians 4:6). Daily prayer together should be a time of enjoyment and praise, which builds an atmosphere of peace in the home.

There are several suggestions we make for couple prayer time. We advise making time together in the morning if at all possible. Praying together while still snuggled in bed is wonderful because it bonds you spiritually as well as meeting each others need for affection. It will set you both on the same page when you communicate throughout the day, as well as when obstacles may arise. If morning is not possible, pray together as soon as you can.

We also recommend husband and wife each takes turns, going back and forth praying for anything that comes to his or her heart. Some of the things we typically cover in our prayer times are:

- Thanksgiving for what the Lord has done for us and those around us,
- Positive and uplifting prayers for each others day,
- Prayer for each other and our children's protection and wisdom,
- Prayer for each other's extended family (parents, siblings, nieces, and nephews),

- Prayer for those in authority over us: our President, nation, military, and employer,
- Prayer for our church and the marriages the Lord puts on our heart.

There are several things we caution couples of during prayer. First, do not use this as a time to criticize each other. We once had a couple say to us, "This prayer together just doesn't work." When we inquired as to why, we found out they ended up fighting every time because they would pray for the other one to grow or change in whatever areas they felt they didn't measure up. We should leave our prayer time together feeling positive and built-up in the Lord.

Second, remember not to criticize each other's families. Prayer for one another's extended family should be done with kindness and love. When we pray for family in a positive way, thanking and trusting God to minister to them and meet their needs, we will begin to look at our spouse's family as our own. We will then see that our spouse loves our extended family as unconditionally as we do, which also builds unity.

Third, know that sometimes couples feel awkward when they first begin to pray together. It is just like learning to ride a bicycle when you were a child. Sometimes it was difficult to get up and moving, but you eventually learned to balance and ride smoothly. So it is with unified prayer. Don't give up! Practice for short periods of time and be patient with one another.

As we learn to pray together, we will grow in God's kind of love. 1 Corinthians 13:5 states, *"[Love] does not behave rudely, does not seek its own, is not provoked, thinks no evil..."* If we think no evil toward our spouse, then we will be patient as we both grow in our walk with the Lord together. We will choose to believe that they are trying their best and, therefore, we will encourage them when they pray.

This is what we were talking about earlier when we compared unified prayer to a tennis doubles team practicing daily. When we make the effort to get ourselves unified in the small things like daily prayer, trials are much easier to overcome when we encounter them.

If you and your spouse have had challenges with prayer together, don't be discouraged! Just start by praising God together each day and thanking Him for the good things He has done in your life and in the lives of those around you. Focus on His goodness.

SOWING AND REAPING

When God created the world, He put into place a spiritual law called the law of sowing and reaping. We will reap what we sow. This law applies to spiritual matters, emotional matters, and physical matters. A farmer sows seed in the ground and eventually reaps a harvest of what he or she planted. A person sows money in the offering to a church or ministry they support, and God sends them increase through multiple avenues. A person sows their time into reading the Bible and reaps the fruit of faith, wisdom, and understanding which directs their life for earthly and eternal good. Let us look at Galatians 6:7-9:

> **Do not be deceived, God is not mocked; for whatever a man sows, that he will also reap. For he who sows to his flesh will of the flesh reap corruption, but he who sows to the Spirit will of the Spirit reap everlasting life. And let us not grow weary while doing good, for in due season we shall reap if we do not lose heart.**

Therefore, when we sow time to the Spirit each day by obeying the Word through practicing and walking in unity, we are building fruit for eternity. This Scripture also encourages us to be diligent about sowing to the Spirit. In other words, don't practice spiritual unity for a week or two and then forget about it. Strong physical muscles are built steadily and consistently by working out but then must continue to be maintained in order to remain strong. Likewise, strong spiritual unity is built through consistent, daily effort that results in a lifelong bond.

We once heard about a study done that showed the divorce rate among couples who pray together regularly is

1 out of every 1,152. This demonstrates great evidence that praying together provides substantial benefit for building and increasing unity. If you and your spouse currently pray alone, why not draw another step closer to God as well as each other by adding unified prayer to build your relationship even stronger.

Matthew 6:33 states, *"But seek first the kingdom of God and His righteousness, and all these things will be added to you."* When we give Him first place in our marriage relationship, He will add the other things to us by causing us to reap a harvest of spiritual, emotional, and physical unity. We have found the more years we pray together, the more we grow in the rest of our marriage. We enjoy our relationship more now than when we were first married.

Jesus said, *"By this all will know that you are My disciples, if you have love one for another"* (John 13:35). If we can exercise love at home and walk in peace consistently with those closest to us, the world will see we have love for one another.

What a great testimony for unbelievers to see a Christian marriage and home filled with an abundance of love created through spiritual unity. What an excellent testimony it also is for unbelievers to see a marriage healed through a couple turning to God and His Word, building a lasting spiritual bond. As we consistently build marital unity through prayer together, we will find ourselves living in a marital masterpiece more and more.

<u>Praying Together</u>

1. Increases boldness in sharing Christ.

2. Produces unity and like-mindedness.

3. Produces a selfless, giving attitude.

4. A marriage that prays together stays together!

Chapter 3

Love from A Pure Heart

**...For as he thinks in his heart, so is he
(Proverbs 23:7).**

SHAUN: GOD'S GLORY RESTORED IN OUR LIFE

I remember when one of my Bible college professors opened our first class of the year with a glass jar in his hands. He told the class that the jar was symbolic of the glory of God. He began to describe in great detail how perfect things were at the beginning in the Garden of Eden. The class was completely quiet as we heard him elaborate on the glorious beginning Adam and Eve experienced. Suddenly, he picked up a hammer and shattered the glass. He then described with deep compassion how the glory of God was shattered from mankind. He asked, "Have you ever met someone who is a little rough around the edge?" as he pointed to the sharp glass fragment still in his hand. Then he picked up more pieces off the floor and remarked, "Have you ever met someone who is edgy and impatient with people? Or have you known someone who cuts others down with their words, always finding things to ridicule?"

Since sin entered the world with the fall of man, it doesn't take long to look and see what this professor was illustrating. The more someone has experienced sin, the more they develop a sharpness and anger toward people. Whether a person is watching sin through media or experiencing it personally, it is like someone is taking that person's heart each time and pouring sludge into it. The more sludge the heart is filled with, the more the enemy is able to work through a person to try to destroy them and those around them.

Even though God's holiness, His glory, and His perfection were all shattered in the life of man through sin, Jesus came and made a way for God's glory to be completely restored in us when we choose to accept Him and walk in His ways. His ways are clearly laid out for us in Scripture. 1 Peter 1:16 tells us, *"Be holy, for I am holy."* Since we still live in a fallen world, how do we walk in this holiness and love others from a pure heart as Christ loves us?

This is a question many have had, even in the church. Occasionally when we are sharing the love of God with someone and invite him or her to pray the prayer of salvation, they may say something like, "Oh, I can't do that. I'm too sinful. I could never live my life right, the way I would have to in order to be a Christian." Or they may say, "I think God is mad at me. He wouldn't want me after all I've done." What these people are really saying is, "I know God is holy and I also know that in my own strength and ability I have some major imperfections. Therefore, I don't think He would want anything to do with me."

The truth is, God gets great pleasure and glory from taking someone the world has considered a failure and making them into a great success! He enjoys showing Himself strong in the life of anyone who will look to Him and ask for help, because He is no respecter of people. He desires to help everyone, whether they are rich or poor, tall or short, black or white. It makes no difference to Him, but He is a gentleman. He doesn't force Himself or His ways on anyone. He always waits for an invitation. When He gets an invitation, He always shows up immediately. He is always ready and waiting to freely impart His life, love, and holiness into anyone's life that will call upon His name. Let us look at how we are able to partake of His holiness in our own life, which includes loving others with His love.

One of the descriptions we found when we looked up holiness was, "The holy people of God are called to holy living precisely because they have been made holy in Christ. Not as a means to that holiness."[2] Therefore, holiness is not something we can earn. The Bible tells us God alone is holy (see Revelation 15:4). Therefore, we can only be holy as He is holy through having a covenant with Him and receiving His holiness in us.

When we enter into that covenant through repentance of our sins, accepting Jesus as our Lord and Savior, we freely become partakers of His holiness. In other words, He made us holy through Christ when He came to abide in our heart. As a result of His holiness living in us, we then have the power to daily make the choice to walk a life of purity for His glory.

SHAUN AND AMY: A VESSEL FOR
GOD'S HONOR

If you have never asked Christ into your heart, we would encourage you to stop right now and do this with us. All you have to do is acknowledge your need for Him as your Savior, repent of your sins, and invite Him into your life. He will help you to love yourself and love others with His love.

Romans 10:13 says, *"Whoever calls on the name of the Lord shall be saved."* Just pray this from your heart right now,

"Dear God, I believe in my heart that Jesus is Your Son. He died on the cross for me and You raised Him from the dead. Jesus, right now I ask You to forgive me of my sins. I accept You into my heart as my Lord

*and Savior. Please make Yourself real to me and help
me to live for You. In Jesus name, amen."*

If you prayed that prayer and meant it in your heart,
your name has now been written down in what is called the
Lamb's Book of Life. The Bible says angels are rejoicing
over your soul. When you pass on from this earth, you now
have the promise of all eternity in Heaven with the Lord and
with your new family of believers that love you! You are now
a partaker of His holiness and have had all sins completely
removed from you!

Just as salvation is a free gift from God, His holiness is
also free of charge. We cannot earn it, but rather we have
received it freely as part of our salvation. We daily choose to
walk in His holiness, because He has already paid the price
on the cross for us to have the victory in every area of our
life. As Paul encourages in 2 Timothy 2:20-22,

**But in a great house there are not only vessels of
gold and silver, but also of wood and clay, some
for honor and some for dishonor. Therefore, if
anyone cleanses himself from the latter, he will
be a vessel for honor, sanctified and useful for the
Master, prepared for every good work. Flee also
youthful lusts; but pursue righteousness, faith,
love, peace with those who call on the Lord out of
a pure heart.**

His holiness came to dwell in us, making our body the temple of the Holy Spirit who is in us (see 1 Corinthians 6:19). Since we as believers have been made a holy temple for God's glory to abide through His Spirit, we are able to live a holy lifestyle through His power. Instead of conforming to the ways of this world, we transform ourselves daily by the renewing of our mind through reading His Word.

GOD'S TRANSFORMING POWER

One of our favorite testimonies of God's transforming power is from the wife of a couple with whom we are close friends. The husband and wife are both very godly people and wonderful examples of two who live according to God's Word and power. However, the wife grew up in a home where she and her siblings were continually devalued through discouraging words.

She shared with us how she used to suffer from depression so severe that she would get huge welts on her body. Doctors prescribed medications, psychiatrists tried to teach her how to cope, but nothing helped. She often thought suicide might be the best way out. Then one day she committed to make Jesus the Lord of her life, rather than just an acquaintance on Sunday mornings. She dug into His Word and began doing what it said. She chose to stop believing what she had been told all of her life. Instead she came to believe in who God says she is because of what Jesus has done for her.

What was the result of her making the choice to believe the Word and change what she thought about herself in her heart? She had a breakthrough. She stopped believing that she was a failure in life and started walking out her new life in Christ. The depression had to leave because she refused to entertain those old thoughts; the welts on her body disappeared; and her relationships improved immensely.

She has become the woman God called her to be and is now fulfilling her God-given destiny. She is a great wife, mother, and friend who is positive, uplifting, confident, and extremely trustworthy. She is a pillar that can't be shaken because she has received a new and firm foundation for herself through being a person who doesn't just read the Bible but also puts it into practice. Through the help of God, she changed what she believed about herself *in her heart*. King Solomon stated it perfectly when he said, *"For as he thinks in his heart, so is he"* (Proverbs 23:7).

AMY: DESIRING THE THINGS OF GOD

When we asked Jesus into our hearts, we were raised up with Christ. We received a desire to seek the things *"...which are above, where Christ is, sitting at the right hand of God"* (Colossians 3:1). We also received the ability and desire to set our *"...mind on things above, not on things on the earth"* (Colossians 3:2). I remember when I asked Jesus into my heart at the age of 14. I suddenly had a strong desire to start getting up early each morning to read the Bible before going to school. No one ever taught me to do this. God placed the desire in me, and I just responded to it.

When I learned things I didn't know before, I started doing them. I remember one day at the age of 15 when I read in the Bible about tithing for the first time. I asked my mom to explain it to me because I had never heard our church teach on this subject. She told me it was when people gave ten percent of their income to God because the Bible says the first tenth of our income belongs to Him. She also said the tithe is one important way we acknowledge God as first place in our life and that God promises to meet all of our needs when we do this (see Malachi 3:10-11). So at the age of 15, I decided to start tithing ten percent of the income from my part-time position and have continued to ever since. I don't do this out of obligation. I do this because I love God and want to show my thankfulness and trust in Him.

As children of the Most High God, we should want to please our loving Father every day. When we choose to live a life pleasing to Him, we are making ourselves a useful vessel for His power to operate through. Then His glory will be revealed to this world and others will be drawn to His goodness.

One day I had a business appointment scheduled with a young woman. When I met with her, we began to talk about the business as planned. However, right in the middle of the conversation, the young woman looked at me and blurted out, "I need to get my life right with God!"

It turned out the young lady had fallen away from her relationship with God and even used to attend the same church we were going to. God was able to minister to her through this meeting together and the young woman got her life right with God and got back into church. Jesus told us that as believers, we are to be the salt and light of the world (see Matthew 5:13-14). He instructed us to, *"Let your light so shine before men, that they may see your good works and glorify your Father in heaven"* (Matthew 5:16). The young lady did not know I was a Christian, but when we keep an open heart to serve God in whatever opportunity may arise, He is able to work through us.

REIGNITING THE FLAME

You may be thinking to yourself right now, "I used to be excited about God like that, but somewhere along the road I just lost my enthusiasm. I still call myself a Christian, but quite frankly, the things of the world are more exciting to me than the things of God." Well, friend, it doesn't have to be that way for you. You can be more excited about your relationship with God, thirty years after making this commitment, than you were the day you gave your life to Him. This applies to marriages as well.

People often think when they have been married for many years that it just isn't suppose to be as exciting as it was in the honeymoon years because the newness has worn off. This is a lie of the devil and does not have to be true for you! We know couples married twenty, thirty, and forty years who are more excited about their marriage now than they were on their honeymoon. They have better communication, better physical intimacy, more fun activities together, more affection, and most of all a greater spiritual bond than when they first married. God never intends for us to backslide in our relationship with Him, and He also does not intend for us to backslide in our enjoyment of the marriage relationship He created between husband and wife.

What can you do if you have fallen into a lack of desire for the things of God? There is an answer. A lack of desire for the things of God can most often be traced back to a time when someone knew to do something God wanted them to do but chose instead to do what their emotions wanted to do.

For example, when someone chooses to ignore the prompting of the Holy Spirit, they dull themselves to the voice of the Holy Spirit. Then the next time the Holy Spirit says something, it becomes a little bit harder to hear with their spiritual ears what He said. As they disobey more and more, they eventually come to a place where the things of God are just not exciting to them anymore. They feel like they never hear from God, and it is because they have tuned Him out through disobedience.

We cannot selectively choose what we are going to obey or not obey with God's Word and His Spirit's leading if we want to walk in His blessing and hear His voice consistently. Therefore, if this has been the case in your life, just repent of disobedience and ask God to renew in you a clean heart of obedience. Then turn to His Word again, and it will come alive to you as you choose to obey Him and take Him at His Word.

WHO WE ARE IN CHRIST

Friend, if you have a painful or less than perfect background, be encouraged today! As you begin to meditate on who you are in Christ and take possession of the promises in His Word, your life will improve. Allow Him to transform what you think of yourself in your heart. Remember, we don't have to earn God's help. Jesus already paid the price for us so we can freely live in God's goodness and promises.

It is vital to read the Word and invest time daily with the Lord. In addition, we have listed key points from Scriptures for you to personalize and meditate on daily.

<u>Remind yourself continually the Bible says (I am)</u>:

Loved by God. John 3:16

Created in His image. Genesis 1:27

Delivered from the power of darkness through His Son. Colossians 1:13

Forgiven from my sins through Jesus. Colossians 1:14

Able to walk in the fruit of the Spirit which dwells in us when we have accepted Him—love, joy, peace, longsuffering, kindness, goodness, faithfulness, gentleness, and self-control. Galatians 5:22-23

Able to forget the things of my past. Philippians 3:13

Able to forgive others as Christ freely forgave me. Colossians 3:13

Able to love others with the love of God. Colossians 3:14

Walking in the peace of God, which surpasses all understanding. Philippians 4:6-7

More than a conqueror through Christ who loves me. Romans 8:37

Called with a holy calling, according to His purpose and grace through Christ before time began. 2 Timothy 1:9

Saved by grace through faith. Ephesians 2:8

Not of this world. John 17:16

Free from the law of sin and death. Romans 8:2

Redeemed from the hand of the enemy. Psalm 107:2

The righteousness of God through faith in Christ Jesus. Romans 3:22

Reigning in life as a king. Romans 5:17

Healed by His stripes. 1 Peter 2:24

Redeemed from the curse of the law. Galatians 3:13

Blessed with all spiritual blessings in Christ. Ephesians 1:3

His workmanship created in Christ Jesus for good works. Ephesians 2:10

Blessed when I hear the word of God and keep it. Luke 11:28

To always speak and meditate on His Word. Joshua 1:8

Increasing in the knowledge of God. Colossians 1:10

Filled with all joy and peace in believing. Romans 15:13

Giving thanks in everything. 1 Thessalonians 5:18

Sharing Jesus with others. Romans 1:16

Sons (and daughters) of God through faith in Christ Jesus. Galatians 3:26

Walking in newness of life. Romans 6:4

Complete in Him. Colossians 2:10

Strong in the Lord and the power of His might. Ephesians 6:10

Walking in God's favor. Proverbs 12:2

Surrounded with His favor like a shield. Psalm 5:12

Filled with the knowledge of His will in all wisdom and spiritual understanding. Colossians 1:9

Walking by faith, not by sight. 2 Corinthians 5:7

Walking in the wisdom of God. James 1:5

OVERCOMING PAST HURTS

One thing you will discover is the more you learn to receive God's love for you, the more you will be able to give His love to others. Typically those who are hardest on others act this way because they do not like themselves or have never felt loved. We cannot give away something we have not first received. In other words, we can only give pure love if we have first allowed God's love to wash and purify our heart from wrongs that have been done to us.

We have seen that many times people who were abused as children grow up to become verbally or physically abusive to their own spouse and children. In other cases, a person may marry someone who is abusive and by choice go into another bad relationship. It all comes back again to the Scripture, *"As he thinks in his heart, so is he."*

If we will make a conscious choice to stop believing the lies from our past, we will be able to move into the magnificent future God has planned for us. God never wants anyone to go through abuse, but it came into the earth as a result of the fall of man. When we become a new creation in Christ Jesus, God gives us the power to forget our past (see Philippians 3:13). The closer we draw to God and focus on who we are in Him, the more the old nature of the person falls off.

1 Peter 1:22 states, *"Since you have purified your souls in obeying the truth through the Spirit in sincere love of the brethren, love one another fervently with a pure heart."* It is

vital for all of us, especially those who have been through abuse, to purify our soul. Renewing our mind and heart through reading and living the truth of the Bible is essential for a victorious life in Christ.

First, we ask God to help us forgive whoever we have held bitterness or unforgiveness toward. We can forgive a person by faith, even if we do not feel it in our heart at the time. Forgiveness is a choice we make based on God's command for us to forgive others as He has forgiven us. Often the unforgiveness a person has in his or her heart is so painful that it can only be forgiven through the power and strength of God.

Second, make the choice to daily obey the truth and walk in the truth. As 3 John 1:4 says, *"I have no greater joy than to hear that my children walk in truth."* This means we read the Word in order to know the truth and then obey what the Word says. It is important to remember God did not give us instructions in His Word to put us in bondage, but rather to keep us from the bondage that sin, death and destruction bring. When we walk in truth we will intentionally focus on loving others from a pure heart, especially those of our own household. When we can love those closest to us consistently, this shows we have come a long way in our love walk.

Third, we retrain our mind and heart to believe who God says we are in His Word, just as we talked about earlier in this chapter. You can look in the mirror and say, *"I am more than a conqueror through Christ who loves me"* (see

Romans 8:37). God wants you to see yourself as the valuable person He created you to be. Think about this: if you take a 100-dollar bill and crumple it up, spit on it, step on it, and put gum in it so it looks nasty, it does not lose its value. It is still worth 100 dollars no matter how bad it looks. In fact, you can take it to the bank and they will trade it in for a new 100-dollar bill. Our life is the same in God's eyes. No matter what we have done wrong, and no matter what others have done to make us feel like we have no value or worth, it doesn't change our value in God's eyes. He can take all the sorrow and disappointments from our past and make us good as new. You have great value and purpose in His plans here on earth. Jeremiah 29:11 is a promise to you that He has *"...thoughts of peace and not of evil, to give you a future and a hope."*

GOD LOVES YOU VERY MUCH

Friend, God loves you very much and wants to give you a new image of yourself being everything He created you to be. Just as our friend stopped living in the hurt from her past through studying and meditating on the Word, we believe you can and will, too. Remember, John 10:10 tells us it is the thief who comes to steal, kill, and destroy, but Jesus came for you to have life more abundantly. This means He came so you could enjoy life not only in heaven one day when you go to be with Him, but you can even enjoy it here on earth right now.

He has already made a way for us to live out all of His good plans and promises for our life through Jesus bringing His holiness into us. As we realize that we are holy because holiness Himself is living in us and then daily choose to yield to His holiness within us, we will see transformation in our life. We are then able to love others the way Jesus does – from a pure heart.

He who believes in Me, as the Scripture has said, out of his heart will flow rivers of living water (John 7:38).

How to Love From A Pure Heart

1. Ask Jesus into your heart.
2. Choose to be a vessel of honor.
3. Pursue the things of God.
4. Daily meditate on who you are in Christ.
5. Forgive others.

Chapter 4

Communication Connection

…A house divided against a house falls
(Luke 11:17).

Everyone has different communication styles. If we want to be effective in our marriage, it is vital to communicate in a way that our spouse can understand and relate with. This is illustrated well by the following story.

Jack and Ashley began with a good marriage. However, as the years progressed, Ashley found herself becoming increasingly frustrated because she desired to have a weekly date with Jack, but he usually only made time for that every few months after much persistence from Ashley. It wouldn't have been so bad, but in the evening he normally did a lot of work on the computer, then watched TV and didn't want to talk during that time. She got only about 10 to 15 minutes of his undivided attention every few nights. Jack also found himself feeling less desire to be with Ashley because she always wanted to discuss problems and he didn't think they had any, other than wishing she desired intimacy more often.

One day Ashley came to Jack and said "Honey, when you watch those car races on TV, why is it that the car driver has a pit crew that changes the tires on their car after so many miles?" Jack responded, "Because the tires would wear out if they didn't and they would eventually have an accident." Ashley responded, "I feel kind of like a race car. As the head of my home, you do the best you know how to be a good driver. But I feel like I have to drive on bald tires quite often because my driver rarely gives me a pit stop by having a date with me to keep our relationship going strong."

Jack was surprised by Ashley's words. He had not realized that regular dates were that important to her. She had told him over and over, but using a different communication method that he could relate with finally drove it home. From that point on, he made an effort to make time for her each week, and he found her desire for intimacy increased as well.

Ashley had decided to stop blaming and start praying for a way to get through to her husband's heart. Through this, she had come across an important communication technique with men, and an example that her husband could relate with because of his love for auto racing. Word pictures that a person can relate with will often get the point across, just as Jesus used stories to illustrate the truths of God's kingdom.

In the past, Ashley used persistence and nagging to try to get her needs met in their relationship, but it had started to drive her husband away. However, when she realized that she needed to approach communication as Jack being for her rather than against her, she started to communicate effectively. When we approach our spouse as our friend and teammate, reaching for a common goal, we will get our point across in a non-threatening, effective way.

Riding home on an airplane one day, we had a wonderful conversation with a businessman sitting next to us. When he found out that we did marriage ministry, he said he had one bit of advice he would like us to give husbands. He went on to tell us that for many years his wife would ask him to have a weekly date so she could have some communication time with him. With their three children, she felt they rarely had any quality conversation together.

Even though he loved his wife very much, for years he rarely responded to her request of weekly time alone. If they did go out, he was always looking around the restaurant to see if there was anyone with whom he could make a business connection. Then, with a look of deep appreciation he said, "God somehow finally got through to me and showed me what I was doing to my wife. He helped me see that next to Him, she is the most important person in my life and I needed to start acting like it."

They finally started having a date on the same night each week without fail. Now wherever they go, he has eyes only for his wife. He is no longer looking for business connections and acquaintances and is no longer answering the cell phone or pager during her time with him. He said it has greatly improved their marriage, and his wife is so much happier now. Then, with a look of regret he said, "It isn't even difficult to take one night out a week for her! I wish I had known sooner how important it was to a marriage."

Studies show that women have a need to talk at least three times more than men. This need to verbally communicate each day shows why it is so important to a wife that her husband take some time each day to listen to her without doing anything else. It makes a woman feel valued when her husband will just listen. However, it is also important for wives to remember that when a husband gives his wife time, it should not be used to vent all of the problems of the day.

When teaching on this topic at a seminar once, a woman from the audience told us the Lord had put it on her heart that the reason He gave her a greater need to speak was so she would edify her husband with those extra words she speaks and meet his need for respect and appreciation.

CHOOSING THE NARROW GATE

Enter by the narrow gate; for wide is the gate and broad is the way that leads to destruction, and there are many who go in by it. Because narrow is

the gate and difficult is the way which leads to life, and there are few who find it (Matthew 7:13-14).

These Scriptures are of course referring to finding the way to eternal life with God in heaven. Yet it is also important to remember that each of our decisions in life also presents us with the choice of God's way or the world's way, the narrow gate or the broad way. Our style of communication is one of those daily choices we make. Are we going to communicate God's way or the world's way? Are we going to treat our spouse like our friend at all times, or treat them like our enemy some of the time?

Once a family member with whom we were visiting for a few days commented that she had been watching us closely to see if we ever gave each other irritated looks. She said "I've even been watching you when you didn't realize anyone else was in the room, and I haven't found you once looking anything but kindly at each other!" We didn't realize this was supposedly abnormal for married people. It shouldn't be. Our spouse should be our best friend, and we should make every effort to make them feel wonderful and accepted when they are around us.

It may be the easy thing to just treat a spouse with irritation or frustration after having a challenging day at work. But that is part of the broad gate the Bible talks about that is easy to slip into by the flesh. As believers, we have the Holy Spirit to help us walk in love at all times so we can enter through the narrow gate. Jesus made a better way for us to communicate with each other, which is through His unconditional love. Even if our spouse doesn't walk in love toward us, we can choose that, as for us, we will live for God and live pleasing to Him. We are accountable to God for our own actions and our spouse is accountable to God for theirs, so as Romans 12:18 says, *"...as much as depends on you, live peaceably with all men,"* and that "men" most definitely includes our spouse and family!

GOOD COMMUNICATION

What creates good communication that doesn't lead to strife? Matthew 7:1 tells us one of the most important keys. *"Judge not, that you be not judged."* A pastor friend of ours who is extremely kind, considerate, and loving once told us that two important keys he has learned are to never assume anything about anyone, and to always choose to believe the best about everyone. He said even if he sees a friend or acquaintance somewhere and they don't say "Hi!" he will not even allow himself to think that they might be mad at him or that they were being rude. Instead he thinks, "They must be extremely busy to have not said hello." Then he will pray for them that God will meet their needs with whatever is causing them to be so preoccupied, and then he chooses to not think about it again.

This example illustrates an important truth. Some people have communication difficulties with others because they judge the other's intentions or actions incorrectly, rather than expecting the best out of them. If a person chooses to "read in" to others actions and become offended because of it, someone will probably come along and do the same thing to them fairly soon. Sometimes this happens back and forth in a marriage repeatedly and creates havoc. It is wise, rather, to not judge or read into actions. Then others are more likely to give us the same courtesy in return. Let us be abundant in grace and rich in mercy toward others!

Another good communication key is asking instead of telling. In Matthew 7:7 Jesus said, *"Ask, and it will be given to you..."* If we are to give God the courtesy of asking Him for something instead of telling Him to give it to us, shouldn't we pay the same courtesy to our spouse and family? When people feel that others owe them something, they tell them to do things. We should never have the attitude that anyone owes us anything.

While a person can probably get away with this in some situations such as with subordinates at work, it is still not the polite or kind thing to do. Our spouse is not our servant (although we should eagerly serve each other out of love) but rather our companion. When orders are given in a marriage, it quickly turns the relationship from one of love and companionship to one of master and servant and most people don't enjoy a marriage like that.

Even with our children, it is wise to ask them to do things rather than tell them, in order to teach them how to be polite to others. Simple things like asking them to please pass something at the dinner table or to please pick up their toys will help them to understand how to be polite and mannerly.

Asking questions also goes a long way in preventing us from making false accusations. Rather than saying, "You hurt my feelings when you said..." it is wise to say, "Do I understand this correctly? Are you saying...?" Asking questions also opens the door to considering more options when discussing a topic. When facing a challenging situation or communication topic, we can approach the problem by each person patiently discussing options, asking if they might work to remedy the situation.

As we mentioned at the beginning of this chapter, an important key to effective communication is to relate our feelings through a word picture that the other person can relate well with rather than just telling it like it is. Especially when recurring obstacles arise, word pictures are often the best answer. We can pray and ask God for a word picture our spouse will identify with in order to make a lasting impact and permanent change.

We find that God used a word picture through the prophet Nathan to correct King David in 2 Samuel 12:1-7.

Then the lord sent Nathan to David, and he came to him, and said to him: 'There were two

men in one city, one rich and the other poor. The rich man had exceedingly many flocks and herds. But the poor man had nothing, except one little ewe lamb which he had bought and nourished; and it grew up together with him and with his children. It ate of his own food and drank from his own cup and lay in his bosom; and it was like a daughter to him.

And a traveler came to the rich man, who refused to take of his own flock and from his own herd to prepare one for the wayfaring man who had come to him; but he took the poor man's lamb and prepared it for the man who had come to him.'

So David's anger was greatly aroused against the man, and he said to Nathan, 'As the Lord lives, the man who has done this shall surely die! And he shall restore four fold for the lamb, because he did this thing and because he had no pity.'

Then Nathan said to David, 'You are this man!'

God knew it would touch David's heart and lead him to repentance if he illustrated David's sin through a word picture without letting him initially know that he was the one who had committed the sin. God also knew that since David used to be a sheepherder, he would relate well with a story about a lamb. It worked and David repented.

One last key we would offer on being a good communicator is to judge your current communication style and make any necessary adjustments. Matthew 7:17 tells us that *"...every good tree bears good fruit, but a bad tree bears bad fruit."* Is your current communication with your spouse and family producing good or bad fruit? Is communication between you and your loved ones done with love and respect or with harshness and dishonor?

It is important to avoid blaming others for how we communicate. Whenever a conversation becomes heated, we have the opportunity to put either water or fuel on the situation with our words. The Bible says that a soft answer turns away wrath. Let's make a quality decision today to put fires out with our words rather than fuel them.

I was able to learn this through Shaun's example to me in our home. I remember several times early in our marriage when I gave him a provoking comment or acted frustrated about something. He didn't respond in anger. In fact one time he came back to me only a few minutes later and said, "Honey, according to the Bible, my family's condition is a reflection of my leadership. I asked the Lord why you just responded shortly with me and He told me I haven't given you quality time lately. I'm canceling my meeting tonight because I have no business leading anything if my family life isn't in order."

His loving response to my behavior taught me a valuable lesson. I learned that no one else can make me get angry. He certainly could have responded sharply and let it turn into an argument, but he didn't because he is a wise man. Over the years he has allowed God to help him become a good tree that consistently communicates with kindness, bearing good fruit.

When we apply the communication principles God shows us in His Word, we will find ourselves first being an example of God's love to others in our home, and then eventually receiving God's love through them in how they communicate with us also. We most likely married our spouse because we valued them and wanted to be with them forever. Let's show them today that we are still thankful we married them by showing respect and kindness when we communicate!

Communication Connection Keys
1. Don't assume anything without asking.
2. Always expect the best in others.
3. Ask instead of tell.
4. Use word pictures.
5. When communicating, approach your spouse as your friend rather than your opponent.

Chapter 5

How to Resolve Strife and Contention

The beginning of strife is like releasing water; therefore stop contention before a quarrel starts (Proverbs 17:14).

What a great analogy this Scripture gives us! Think of a water dam. If only a small amount of water is trickling through the dam, it is easy to block and stop the flow of water. However, if water is gushing through the dam, it is more difficult to stop the flow. This Scripture tells us to gain control of our tongue at the beginning of a disagreement and work things out peaceably, rather than saying many words and allowing anger to escalate. It is much easier to stop contention before sharp words have started to flow like rushing water.

Have you noticed that when strife and anger start spewing out of someone's mouth, it is rarely in only one or two sentences? In fact, it is usually not even just about the matter at hand that caused the fight. Often, unresolved hurts and issues from the past are also brought up because the fountain of strife is flowing like gushing water that doesn't want to stop. Before we decide to allow contention to out and start striving with someone, it is wise to remember Proverbs 20:3, *"It is honorable for a man to stop striving, since any fool can start a quarrel."*

WHERE DO STRIFE AND FIGHTING COME FROM?

Before we look at how to stop contention before it starts, let us look at where strife and fighting come from. When we as believers truly understand the root cause for strife and fighting, I believe we will be more determined to prevent it from occurring in our relationships. Proverbs 13:10 gives us one great cause of strife. It says, *"By pride comes nothing but strife."* This is one of the root issues – pride. Therefore, it is easy to see that when someone chooses to enter into strife, it is being instigated through the satanic realm.

Satan, who was once called Lucifer, was removed by force from his position in Heaven as one of the head angels because he got into pride and wanted to be God. Therefore, Satan is the author of pride. This is why 1 Peter 5:5 says, *"God resists the proud, but gives grace to the humble."* Until a person is willing to humble himself or herself, God will not show up on their behalf. Why? When a person gets into pride, he or she is submitting to the lordship of Satan rather than the Lordship of Jesus.

As a person causes or participates in strife, they are also neglecting Jesus' command quoted in John 15:12: *"This is my commandment, that you love one another as I have loved you."* An excellent example of this is shown in Proverbs 10:12, *"Hatred stirs up strife, but love covers all sins."* Therefore, if we participate in strife we are choosing to walk in Satan's realm, which is hatred, rather than walking in Christ's command of love. Knowing this, it is not any surprise that James said, *"For where envying and strife is, there is confusion and every evil work"* (James 3:16, KJV). If we choose to walk in strife, we are also choosing to open the door to the devil, giving him free reign to bring confusion and every evil thing into our life.

James had quite a bit to say about fighting and disagreements. In James 4:1-3 he states that fighting comes from a person's desire for pleasure, which is rooted in lust and coveting. When someone lusts or covets after something they don't have, that is ultimately from pride because they are saying that what God has given them isn't good enough. A classic example of this is King David. We find the story in 2 Samuel 11:2-4,

And from the roof he saw a woman bathing, and the woman was very beautiful to behold. So David

sent and inquired about the woman. And someone said, 'Is this not Bathsheba, the daughter of Eliam, the wife of Uriah the Hittite?' Then David sent messengers, and took her; and she came to him, and he lay with her . . .

The story continues with David later having her husband killed because she was pregnant with King David's baby. After he committed this great wickedness, he was visited by Nathan the prophet and rebuked by God. The Lord said to David,

I gave you your master's house and your master's wives into your keeping, and gave you the house of Israel and Judah. And if that had been too little, I also would have given you more! (2 Samuel 12:8).

It is interesting to note that in addition to addressing David's act of adultery, God also went on to address David's lack of contentment with what he already had as sinful behavior. Hebrews 13:5 advises us, *"Let your conduct be without covetousness; be content with such things as you have."* God had given David so many good gifts and even with all that he possessed, he became discontented, lusting and coveting after what belonged to someone else.

This is how pride and selfishness work. No matter how much God gives someone they are not appreciative for what they do have. A person who allows pride and selfishness to rule their life will never be consistently satisfied with anything or anyone emotionally, physically, or sexually. This is why prideful people are often angry people. They are especially good at putting on a facade for those outside their family, yet they get into strife and snap at those of their own household without apology.

People living this way often don't know why they are angry so often. It is because they have yielded to pride and selfishness and this causes a recurring dissatisfaction because nothing ever seems good enough. There may be a few temporary moments of satisfaction where pride feels a short-lived fix. A big achievement, a promotion, purchasing a new top-of-the-line car, watching pornography, or an illicit sexual encounter may give short gratification, but then the dissatisfaction is right back again and the person lashes out in anger at those they are closest to.

It is not wrong to desire something, as long as it is not against Biblical principles to have what we desire. Psalm 37:4 says *"Delight yourself also in the Lord, and He shall give you the desires of your heart."* The true test is, do we invest more time thinking about how good God has been to us and how we can be a gift to others or do we invest in thinking about what we don't have.

79

The good news is, if we realize that pride has been leading us, we can repent and choose to change our ways just like David did. Isaiah 55:7 gives us a wonderful description of God's mercy, saying, *"...Let him return to the Lord, and He will have mercy on him, and to our God, for He will abundantly pardon."*

God only shows us what we need to change in ourselves because He loves us and He knows that we don't have to live a life of discontentment. He has already provided a way for all of our needs to be met and for us to have divine satisfaction when we walk with a thankful heart toward Him for the things we do have. True satisfaction comes from knowing the grass isn't any greener on the other side; rather, it's greenest where it is best watered and properly tended to.

IS STRIFE EVER GOOD?

We have heard it said that a certain amount of strife and fighting is necessary and healthy for a marriage. It is just like the devil to try to feed the world and the body of Christ a lie like this to get people right where he wants them, having an open door to bring destruction into their life and family. Good communication to help resolve disagreements is necessary and healthy for a marriage, but strife and fighting is not good, according to the Word. Let us look at several more references to reiterate that strife and fighting are not from God, and therefore, not good:

He who has knowledge spares his words, and a man of understanding is of a calm spirit (Proverbs 17:27).

A fool takes no pleasure in understanding, but only in expressing his opinion (Proverbs 18:2, RSV).

The discretion of a man makes him slow to anger, and his glory is to overlook a transgression (Proverbs 19:11).

Be angry and do not sin, do not let the sun go down on your wrath, nor give place to the devil (Ephesians 4:26-27).

To understand what strife does to a relationship, picture a horizontal pole with a bucket on each end. The weight of the first bucket represents God's ability to help us in our marriage and family, while the weight of the second bucket represents Satan's ability to harm us and bring destruction into our life and family. When we speak loving, respectful, complimentary words to our spouse and children, it fills up God's bucket to work on our behalf. However, if we speak angry, rude, demanding, or hurtful words to our spouse and family, it fills up Satan's bucket to bring harm and destruction to us.

This is how Satan works on a marriage or relationship. If we give him a place in our marriage or family through strife or unresolved anger, he then has access to steal, kill, and destroy (see John 10:10).

It is important to note there is another type of anger the Bible refers to which is a righteous anger. Jesus became angry at sin, such as when He overturned the moneychangers' tables in the temple (see Matthew 21:12). This was directed at sinful behavior because God is good and He hates sin. There are times in a believer's life when it is right for us to have anger if it is a righteous anger. For example, a believer should get angry about the devil trying to bring destruction into their life. James 4:7 tells us *"Submit to God. Resist the devil and he will flee from you."*

If a person doesn't have a righteous anger about the works of darkness in their own life or the lives of others, they will probably not pray as fervently as they need to in order to change the situation. This type of anger typically is not directed at a person but at a situation. There were times when Jesus became righteously angry about something, and He occasionally verbalized this anger, particularly with those religious people who claimed to serve God but really didn't with their hearts. However, most often we find his righteous anger causing Him to more fervently pursue destroying the works of darkness through ministering healing and miracles to those who were bound by Satan.

STEPS TO RESOLVE CONTENTION

Some people avoid discussing their problems altogether because they are afraid it will lead to strife. This is especially common when someone with a passive personality is married to someone with a direct personality. Passive people tend to despise confrontation, while direct people often enjoy it. For this reason, many passive people would rather let their frustration or hurt feelings build up inside of them than confront an issue so they don't risk making anyone mad. In these situations, when a passive person allows unresolved anger to build up and continues to not deal with it, their spouse sometimes gets a huge surprise one day when they suddenly erupt like a volcano or walk out on the relationship.

On the opposite side, it is often difficult for people with dominant personalities to address areas of contention without it turning into strife. Dominant people tend to be competitive by nature and often enjoy debate because it is a form of competition. It is important for dominant people to remember there is a time and place for competition, but it is not in the marriage relationship over differences of opinion that could hurt their spouse's feelings.

In this section it is our goal to give steps based on Scripture that will allow couples of every personality type to resolve areas of contention peacefully and diffuse anger, in a spirit of love and kindness. These steps are best when used by both husband and wife. However, they are still helpful when used by just one person in the couple as well.

In looking at scriptural steps to resolve contention, let us go back to Proverbs 17:14, *"The beginning of strife is like releasing water; therefore stop contention before a quarrel starts."* If Solomon said to stop contention before it starts, certainly he knew there was a way to do this. The original Hebrew word used for contention actually means controversy (Strong's #7379). Therefore, Solomon was saying that when someone has controversy with another person, which means to have differing or opposing viewpoints, rather than letting it turn into an escalation of anger that results in a fight, we should deal with the opposing viewpoints in a manner that will bring peace and resolution rather than anger and division.

How does God instruct us to stop contention before it escalates to heated anger and fighting? Let us look at James's answer to this question. Notice that he starts Chapter Four by saying, *"Where do wars and fights come from among you?"* He did not say, "Where do wars and fights come from among people?" He specifically said *among you*, which means this was written to Christians. Therefore, he is addressing wars and fights among believers. James goes on to tell us the key to eliminating these fights. He says the key is humbling ourselves so that God can lift us up. As we mentioned earlier, James informs us that one way to show humility is by submitting to God and resisting the devil.

We have personally found in our own marriage and in couples we have worked with over the years, one of the best ways to humble ourselves before God during an issue of contention is by humbly praying together. Throughout Jesus' time on earth, He continually went to God to gain strength and direction through prayer. If we follow Christ's example when contention and opposing viewpoints arise, we will also gain strength from God to walk in His love toward our spouse and receive direction to resolve the conflicting opinions.

Let us give you an example. When we even sense an opposing viewpoint on something that has any potential for becoming an argument, one of us says, "Let's stop and pray over this." Then we don't say another word until we hold hands and say a prayer such as,

"Lord, we commit our conversation and our thoughts to You right now. We pray that You would help us to discuss this in a spirit of love, and to be kind and considerate with each other. We ask that You help both of us see this from Your viewpoint and please help us to come to a quick resolution of this issue that will be pleasing to You. In Jesus name, amen."

We can personally say that every time we have done this, God has intervened and helped us to walk in love so the contention did not escalate to anger. In our years of marriage, we can count on one hand the number of times we have gotten into a disagreement where our words effected each other in a negative way. Each of the few times this has happened has only been when neither of us stopped to suggest we pray.

Our being able to talk things out and resolve contention peacefully is definitely not because we have a special gift from God to be patient or that we are just passive and don't like to stand up for what we believe. Neither of us is passive, and we have no difficulty verbalizing our thoughts. We have simply learned to follow His Word in regard to handling contention, and He is faithful to help us resolve any issue that may arise.

When we teach about praying to help resolve contention at marriage seminars, a common question is, "What if you are already feeling angry? How do you get yourself to stop and pray with your spouse?" The answer we have is this: you just have to make the choice to do it by faith. We have clearly seen that stopping yourself to pray is much easier for those who invest at least some amount of time daily with the Lord and Bible reading because they have practiced discerning their senses to the Holy Spirit's leading.

SHAUN: MORE ON RESOLVING CONTENTION

I have even used this approach to resolve contention at a Christian work environment and seen it work miracles. I remember one time when I had brought a polite correction to another believer who had a direct personality and who worked with me at the time. He got angry about what I said and came to see me. He verbalized his anger, telling me I had no business correcting him.

I first apologized for offending him, then said, "You know, we are both believers, so how about if we just bring this to the Lord right now and ask Him to help us resolve it?" The man was surprised by my response and said, "Well, okay." I prayed and asked God to help us resolve the issue in a spirit of love and unity as our employer would want us to, and then he prayed a few things after me. When we finished, his anger had completely subsided. He said a few nice things to me and left. God is faithful to perform His Word! When we humble ourselves by submitting to Him and resisting the devil, God pours His grace out on the situation, and the devil really does have to flee!

A second step to resolving conflict peacefully is found in Proverbs 15:1, *"A soft answer turns away wrath, but a harsh word stirs up anger."* This principle is a miracle worker when someone is upset. In the story I just shared about my former coworker, if I had instead chosen to respond back with contention, voicing my opinion on the matter and insisting I was right, the situation most likely would have escalated to strife.

When giving a soft answer, it is sometimes necessary to apologize for making someone feel offended or however they say our actions or words made them feel. Even if we do not believe that what we said or did was wrong, we still should not want to offend someone. When we act in humility toward someone who is upset with us, it will most often diffuse the anger like popping air out of a balloon.

The third step in handling contention can usually be done quite easily if the first two steps of humbling ourselves through prayer and using a soft answer are followed. This step is to yield to God's wisdom in resolving the issue of disagreement. James 3:17 tells us how this wisdom operates:

But the wisdom that is from above is first pure, then peaceable, gentle, willing to yield, full of mercy and good fruits, without partiality and without hypocrisy.

SHAUN AND AMY: WISDOM KEYS TO DISCUSS A MATTER

Each of the words in James 3:17 give us direction as to how wise conflict resolution is attained. *Pure* means to be clean and unmixed with other matters. Therefore, when we discuss the issue of disagreement, we should not bring up anything else. We don't talk about or allow ourselves to think about past hurts or mistakes. We only discuss the matter at hand. If someone brings up other issues from the past, we are not allowing ourselves to come to quick resolution of the matter at hand because we just stirred up more problems.

Many years ago, Amy heard a very gifted Christian counselor speak at a church. He said when he was a boy he had several very traumatic things happen to close family members. As a young adult, he came to the realization that there are two kinds of people in life and he had to choose which one he was going to be. He said there are those who keep a bucket of horse manure with them everywhere they go. Every time something bad happens, it adds another scoop of manure to their bucket. They carry the bucket with them and show it to those they encounter. They stir it in front of people to make sure it stays fresh and everyone gets a whiff of how bad it smells.

On the opposite side, there are others who take the manure bucket and dump it out to fertilize their garden. They know bad things don't come from God, but rather from the devil. Therefore, they have determined in their hearts they will not carry a bucket of manure around by meditating repeatedly on their past hurts. This man said he chose at a young age to be the second kind of person. He had a life filled with joy because he had chosen to look to the future. He became a counselor because he wanted to help others stop stirring their bucket of manure and rather start fertilizing their gardens so those around them could smell roses instead of manure.

We share this story to illustrate what it is like if someone brings up past hurts or mistakes in a time of conflict resolution. If someone brings up the past, it is typically because they have unforgiveness that has not been dealt with. Therefore, they want to stir their manure and make the other person suffer a while by having to smell the stench of it. Instead of doing this, let us choose to be pure in our conflict resolution and not mix the matter at hand with anything else from the past.

The other words James uses to describe godly wisdom are also extremely important in resolving contention. He says to be *peaceable* which means discussing the matter without raising our voice. Therefore, we just choose not to allow ourselves to escalate to anger. If a person has a continual problem with anger, it is helpful to read the Word more often throughout the day, attend Christian-based classes to help with this issue, as well as ask the Lord to remove the anger from your heart.

James goes on to mention being gentle and willing to yield. The word *gentle* here also means patient (Strong's #1933). Someone being *willing to yield* means they are willing to consider the other person's view. Wisdom is also without *partiality*, which means we do not automatically give preference to our own opinion, but rather we are willing to give equal consideration to another's viewpoint as long as it doesn't disagree with the Bible.

Many people tell us finances are a frequent area of contention in their marriage. One easy way to minimize many financial disagreements is to make and stay accountable to a budget. If you have not done this, we would encourage you to start a budget immediately.

Most disagreements revolve around the statement of, "Let's buy this certain item right now." A budget will often stop these disagreements because you then go as a couple and look at the budget. If the price of the item is not in the budget previously agreed upon, then it is not the spouse saying no, it is the budget saying no. Many couples make purchases because they "feel" like they can afford it. Finances are not based on feelings. If the budget doesn't allow for the purchase, then make it a faith project the two of you believe for together.

GODLY COMMUNICATION

In His Word God has laid out a plan for us to have peaceful homes, free from strife and fighting. His desire is for you and your family to have peace and unity so that He can have free reign to bring life and blessing to all of you. If strife has been a challenge in your relationships, know it is worth the effort to continually practice these steps to resolve contention. You may even want to write out the Scriptures from this chapter and keep them in a place where you will see them often. The more we get His Word into our mind and heart about this topic, the easier it will be to apply it when contention arises.

We have consistently seen that when couples follow God's Word for guidance in Godly communication and elimination of strife, marriages are much more enjoyable and productive. A couple who knows how to maintain peace and unity in their home is better able to lay hold of and fulfill the plans God has for them. We know God has good plans for you as a couple. Now that we have discussed how to maintain peace in the home, let us go on to the next step in communication, which is presenting our words as a gift!

Keys To Resolving Strife

1. Stop strife before it can start by humbly praying together, asking for God's help.
2. Remember strife comes from a prideful attitude.
3. Remember avoiding strife prevents confusion and other evil works from entering your life.
4. Choose to forgive past hurts and only discuss the matter at hand.

Chapter 6

Present Your Words as a Gift

**Pleasant words are like a honeycomb, sweetness
to the soul and health to the bones
(Proverbs 16:24).**

W hen doing marriage seminars, we typically give a sheet of paper for each person to fill out at one of the sessions, asking them to list five things they most appreciate about their spouse. Then they are supposed to give the list to their spouse. Numerous times, we have had women in particular tell us afterward that when they read their husband's list about them they cried. These women expressed how they had never heard their husband say these things before, and seeing them in writing brought them to tears. It seems couples often think the other one "just knows" they are appreciated. However, how can they know unless they are told?

Just think how powerful and impacting it would be on every marriage if spouses, parents, and children verbalized the things they appreciate about each other on a daily basis. We believe this alone would drop the divorce rates drastically and cause children to do better in school! People have a need to feel significant and do something significant. Interestingly, the more valued someone feels, the more likely they are to accomplish great things. Later in this chapter we will show you why.

Our words have great power to set the course of direction for those under our sphere of influence. Often without realizing it, we are making the choice each day to speak words that heal or words that hurt. When we speak pleasantly to those around us, it literally brings health to their body! Have you ever noticed people will often gravitate toward someone who makes them feel good about themselves? Why? Good words refresh the human spirit. When we hear kind words spoken over us it actually empowers us to live a healthy, prosperous life. Similarly, when we speak words of praise and thankfulness to God and others, we are veered away from defeat and propelled toward victory.

There was a study done on women who left their husband before no-fault divorce laws. It showed the top reason wives walked away from their marriage was that they felt unappreciated. If the same study had been done on men, I'm sure the results would have been similar, because everyone needs to feel valued. Mary Kay Ash used to say, make people feel like they are wearing a sign that says, "Make me feel important!"

THE POWER OF PRAISE

We can learn so much about having an effective marriage and family from observing Christ's relationship with the church and the church's relationship with Christ. In the Book of Acts, Chapter 16, we find the account of Paul and Silas being thrown into prison. It tells us in verses 25-26,

But at midnight Paul and Silas were praying and singing hymns to God, and the prisoners were listening to them. Suddenly there was a great earthquake, so that the foundations of the prison were shaken; and immediately all the doors opened and everyone's chains were loosed.

At this point of great trial and affliction, Paul and Silas chose to respond through prayer and praise! This was truly what Psalm 116:17 calls offering to God *"...the sacrifice of thanksgiving."* It isn't that God needs our praise at times of trial and despair in our life. We need to praise Him in order to get our mind off our circumstances and on God's ability to show up on our behalf. When Paul and Silas did this, they were not only loosed from their chains and jail cell, but all of the other prisoners were loosed also! This shows a very important spiritual point; our praise has the ability to not only set us free from the power of darkness, but others as well.

We find another account of the power of praise in 2 Chronicles 20:21-22:

And when he had consulted with the people, he appointed those who should sing to the Lord, and who should praise the beauty of holiness, as they went out before the army and were saying: 'Praise the Lord, for His mercy endures forever.' Now when they began to sing and to praise, the Lord set ambushes against the people of Ammon, Moab, and Mount Seir, who had come against Judah; and they were defeated.

Praise is powerful! Praise breaks the strongholds of the enemy. God was able to move on His people's behalf to defeat their enemies because they put their faith and trust in Him through praise! God is the same yesterday, today, and forever. He will show Himself strong on our behalf just as powerfully today when we praise Him and even more so now because we have a covenant through Jesus.

When we are in a difficult situation, whether it be marriage, children, or anything else, we can praise Him because He is faithful! We can praise Him because His mercy endures forever! After we pray faith-filled and Holy-Spirit-led prayers over our situation, we can praise and thank Him that He is going to take what the devil intended for our harm and turn it around for our good and His glory (see Romans

8:28). We can believe God that when the dust settles, we will still be standing and we will be all the stronger in our walk with God and in our relationships!

David was called a man after God's own heart, and we see why in the book of Psalms. He was constantly praising God. In fact, Psalm 119:164 tells us he praised the Lord seven times a day! If something bad happened, He praised God for being faithful and merciful. If something good happened, he praised Him for the good.

No matter what, David was always praising! He even said when he was going through a great trial of affliction, *"But I will hope continually, and will praise You yet more and more"* (Psalm 71:14). In other words, the devil just couldn't shut him up. He was determined to praise no matter what! You know, you just can't keep a man like that down. One way or another he is going to rise to the top because God inhabits the praises of His people. God will do the same thing for us. Our praise to God has the ability to completely turn a situation around. As Psalm 100:4 says, *"Enter His gates with thanksgiving, and into His courts with praise."*

PRESENTING YOUR WORDS AS A GIFT

The church has great success with answered prayers from God when they praise Him. Praise in marriage produces similar results. For this reason, it is helpful to think of our words and actions to our spouse and family as a gift. If what we are about to say or the facial expression we may be tempted to give is not like a beautifully wrapped gift to present to our spouse or children, we should choose not to give it to them! Only present words, expressions, and actions that are like a beautiful gold package with a shiny bow on top. When we make our words a gift, we are placing value on our spouse and children, rather than devaluing them. Then, even our daily interactions become an investment in our future together and create an atmosphere of peace in our home. As Ephesians 4:29 tells us,

Let no corrupt word proceed out of your mouth, but what is good for necessary edification, that it may impart grace to the hearers.

Notice that it describes edification as necessary. When something is necessary it means it is absolutely essential and vitally important. Edifying and building up those we love is essential to their well-being. When we build up our spouse and children with words, we empower them to prosper and empower our relationship with them to prosper! This Scripture also says that when we edify someone, we impart grace to the one we are speaking to. The word interpreted as grace is originally the Greek word "charis," which means, "divine influence upon the heart, and its reflection in the life; including gratitude" (Strong's #5485). Our words we speak to our family are awesomely powerful! When we edify and show gratitude to those close to us, we are actually bringing God's divine influence to work upon their heart, which will then be reflected in their life!

Since other's words have so much influence in our life, our tendency as humans, especially in children, is to gravitate toward those who make us feel good about ourselves. Benjamin Franklin, once the American Ambassador to France renowned for his excellent people skills, addressed the importance of not criticizing, but rather lavishing praise in this way, "I will speak ill of no man, and speak all the good I know of everybody."

BENEFITS OF PRAISE

Praise benefits the giver as well as the receiver. When someone focuses on consistently giving sincere praise to others, they are protecting themselves from a heart of ungratefulness. Romans 1:21 tells of what happens to the heart of people who are ungrateful.

...Although they knew God, they did not glorify Him as God, nor were thankful, but became futile in their thoughts, and their foolish hearts were darkened.

We see from this Scripture that the key to having a pure heart (both with God and our marriage) is to keep a continual heart of thankfulness. Genuine appreciation and thankfulness is also a good way to stay humble. People who don't want to give others praise or appreciation are often people who like to talk and boast about themselves. Pride likes to focus on self, while humility is glad to let others have the spotlight. When we choose to consciously look for good in others and verbalize this to them, we guard our own heart from growing cold toward the person. Likewise, as we glorify and thank God, we guard our heart from growing cold toward Him and His Word.

Sometimes people may be concerned about praising their spouse or other family members, wondering if this will make the other person prideful because of being edified often. In fact, some people even purposefully insult others or even laugh when their children insult each other, thinking it will keep them humble or callous them to better handle the "real world." This is actually an attack of the devil, intended to greatly damage and destroy a spouse or child's confidence.

Satan knows if he succeeds in destroying a person's confidence through those who supposedly love them the most, it will cause the adult or child to feel inferior and inadequate to accomplish what God has called them to. This will often steal their God-given destiny from being fulfilled. Anyone who has been greatly successful in life will tell us that a person still gets much farther ahead in the "real world" through praising others than by criticizing.

When edification is done in the right way, which includes encouraging and building a person up for who God made them to be, pride should not become a factor in a person's life. In fact, edification should even bring out humility when a person is complimented for who he or she is in Christ.

A good example of this used to happen to Amy in her childhood. Whenever someone would compliment her appearance as a little girl, her mother would immediately respond by saying to the person, "Thank you! And what's most important is that she's just as pretty on the inside!" Because of this, Amy grew up with the mindset of knowing that being kind to people was of utmost importance. Her mother wanted her to grow up knowing a kind personality is more important than looks. When a parent gives a child compliments on their kindness toward others, the child will make even more effort to be this way!

The Bible admonishes us of the importance of building one another up in 1 Thessalonians 5:11, which states, *"Therefore comfort [encourage] each other and edify one another..."* Interestingly, the original word translated as edify here actually means "to be a house builder, to construct, confirm, build up, and embolden" (Strong's #3618). This is profound! When we edify and encourage those of our household, we are being a house builder! With our words of edification and praise, we are inspiring them to go forth in courage and become all God has called them to be! As we edify those we love, we actually construct a foundation in them and with them that will endure the test of time and trials!

AMY: WASHING OTHERS WITH OUR WORDS

For men and women alike, praise has a profound effect on making people feel loved and appreciated. Ephesians 5:25-27 states,

Husbands, love your wives, just as Christ also loved the church and gave Himself for her, that He might sanctify and cleanse her with the washing of water by the word, that He might present her to Himself a glorious church, not having spot or wrinkle or any such thing, but that she should be holy and without blemish.

This tells us that a husband is to love his wife the same way Christ loves the church. According to this Scripture, one of the ways Christ loves the church is by cleansing her with His Word, which removes the church's spots and wrinkles and causes her to become glorious. From this, we know that a husband must also have the same ability to "wash" his wife with his words of kindness to help remove "spots" from her personality.

One of the best illustrations we have of this happened in our own life some years ago. I had been very busy for several weeks and had let the laundry (which is one of the things I choose to do in the home) pile up extremely high. When Shaun got home one night, I apologized for his having hardly any clean clothes. I told him I was tired and had been so busy lately that I hadn't been keeping up with this chore. He could tell I felt very overworked, overwhelmed, and didn't have a good attitude about the task ahead of me.

When a husband sees his wife with a bad attitude about something, they can do one of several things. First, they can be hard on their wife about her attitude or her negligence in getting the task done. Second, they can be indifferent to the situation, say that's fine, and go on to another topic. Third, they can respond the way Shaun did with me that night, by washing their wife with their words.

Shaun gave me a big smile and said, "Oh honey, I understand you've had a lot on your plate. You work so hard for us, and I appreciate the things you do for our family so much. I don't know what I would do without you. You make our home such a peaceful place to live. That laundry isn't a big deal. I'll help you with it this weekend. You do a great job as a wife, and I'm so thankful for you." My attitude changed instantly from overwhelmed to optimistic! I no longer felt inadequate. I was so inspired by his appreciation that I cheerfully went and completed the task of doing all the laundry. His words of praise washed my attitude of its wrinkles and made me feel loved and appreciated.

A wife's words have a similar impact on her husband because words of praise, admiration, and thankfulness are all part of showing respect. Ephesians 5:33 tells us,

...Let each one of you in particular so love his own wife as himself, and let the wife see that she respects her husband.

It is important to remember, however, that praise and respect are not something we only give when we want something done. We should show respect and praise consistently, on a daily basis, because it is the right thing to do and because we love our spouse. Everyone likes to feel appreciated. Even God enjoys appreciation, and we are made in His image. It is not much fun doing things for someone who is ungrateful, but it is inspiring when someone gives us praise because it is a motivating force!

When a husband does something around the house, whether big or small, a wife should always take note of it, verbally praising and appreciating him. When a woman focuses on the things her husband does, rather than what he doesn't do, the wife will find that he enjoys helping much more. For example, a wife may ask her husband to do something like paint a room. If he doesn't do it immediately, a wife may often resort to nagging. However, the wise thing for her to do would be to simply make a lifestyle of praising him for everything he does do. She could thank him for going to work for the family, taking out the trash, washing the car, taking the family out to eat, or anything else she can think of. When a husband feels appreciated, he is much more likely to be helpful because of the wife showing respect.

God intended for a wife to be her husband's biggest encourager and vice versa. There are times when a husband knows he is called to do something, but it is the wife's encouragement and belief in him and his God-given abilities that give him the needed push to fulfill his God-given destiny.

We once heard a man tell how he had started a ministry under the direction of God, but a few years into it things became very tough. He wanted to give up but asked his wife what she thought. She reminded him of everything the Lord had previously shown them regarding the ministry. She spoke confidently of attaining a successful future and cheered him on, knowing it was God's plan to persevere. Her words brought new stamina and endurance to him for running the race, and with God's help the ministry was a success. This wife understood the importance of honoring and encouraging her husband and lived like the woman in Proverbs 31:26: *"She opens her mouth with wisdom, and on her tongue is the law of kindness."*

Whether it is encouraging our spouse regarding their calling in life, or being appreciative to our family for the little things they do around the house, it is important we remember to be someone who lavishes praise on others. When we are consistent with our praise, we build an atmosphere of peace in our home and also bring out the best in those around us. Criticism destroys a relationship, but sincere praise brings life and health. As we freely give praise and appreciation to our spouse and family, we are being a wise "house builder" and will see the fruit from our words being "sweet to their soul and health to their bones!"

The Words We Speak

1. Always present your words as a gift.
2. Remember to verbalize your appreciation.
3. Praise God in the midst of trials and your breakthrough will come.
4. Praising God and others helps us keep a humble heart.
5. Kind words bring life and blessing to others.

Chapter 7

Submission Creates Equality

But I want you to know that the head of every man is Christ, the head of woman is man, and the head of Christ is God (1 Corinthians 11:3).

When the Lord spoke to our hearts about writing a book on marriage, He very specifically gave us the title for this chapter. The word "submission" has been so abused and misunderstood that many Christians do not want to talk about it, men and women alike. For lack of knowledge on genuine Christ-like submission, numerous Christian marriages have failed between well-meaning, God-loving couples.

We have all heard stories of men who have tried to *make* their wives submit by commanding her to do so. Likewise, we have all heard tales of wives who have avoided submission. A woman may think she makes a "better person in charge" than her husband, or may possibly fear that submission would put her at a lower status than her husband, becoming a doormat to be stepped on and taken advantage of.

The good news about submission is that God's way of doing things is always best for both husband and wife because He is a righteous and loving God! If we truly understand *how much God loves us*, we will know and believe that He had both the husband and wife's best interest in mind when He planned the marriage union this way. Therefore, God is not favoring men because He instructed them to be the head of the home. Likewise, women are not less in God's eyes because He asked them to be the ones to submit to their husband. God simply knew that one body with two heads is a monster! When a husband and wife are joined by His supernatural power into one at their marital union, together they have become one body in Christ.

As Eve was taken out of Adam, God made it essential for the two to work in unity with each other in order to be effective in taking dominion in the earth. This body of one, when working together properly, reflects God's goodness and His glory. The divine interdependence and unity necessary to have an effective, rewarding relationship involves the husband cleaving (being joined) to his wife and the wife submitting to her husband. When the husband is joined to the wife, as Christ is joined and committed to the church, and the wife submits to her husband, as the church is to submit to Christ, this union is strong and powerful, the way God intended it to be.

God also planned submission because He knew the marriage body would need to have order to be most effective. Order is created through having levels of submission. Genesis 2:21-24 tells us God created man first and then woman came out of man.

And the Lord God caused a deep sleep to fall on Adam, and he slept; and He took one of his ribs, and closed up the flesh in its place. Then the rib which the Lord God had taken from the man He made into a woman, and He brought her to the man. And Adam said, 'This is now bone of my bones and flesh of my flesh; she shall be called Woman, because she was taken out of man.'

For this reason, the husband is the one God placed as the head because the woman came from the man. As spiritual beings in Christ, man and woman are created equal. This equality, however, does not nullify the system of authority God ordained to keep the home in order. God, in His great wisdom, planned leadership to bring order and unity to the home. Through Scripture, we will show you how He also planned submission to create equality in the marital relationship.

SHAUN AND AMY: COVENANT
RELATIONSHIP

Before we discuss what true submission is and how it brings about equality, we must first have understanding of the marriage covenant relationship. Man and woman were created by God to have interdependence in their marriage union in order for them to be the most effective on the earth. When we study covenant relationships throughout history, we discover that once a covenant is entered into, everything one person has also belongs to the other person, and vice versa. Likewise, in the marriage covenant, everything of who we are, what we have been gifted with, what we own or owe, everything good or bad, all becomes our spouse's as well as our own. Entering a marriage covenant means our spouse now has equality with us as covenant partners. In a covenant, there is no such thing as this is mine and this is yours.

Often, people from African cultures tend to understand the meaning of covenant better than people of other nations. In Africa, if a tribal leader enters into covenant with someone, each of the people exchange a most treasured possession to signify their covenant. Knowing the protection a tribal leader can give, a missionary may go to a tribal leader in the area and ask to make a covenant with him. If the leader agrees, they will enter into covenant and then exchange something that is precious to each of them. The tribal leader may give the missionary his staff, which is a symbol of his authority.

Thereafter, if the same missionary is out and about, no one will dare lay a hand on him or any of his belongings. If they did, the tribal leader and all his warriors would come and fight for him and see to it that what was stolen is restored to him.

It is very similar to what we read in Genesis 14:14-16 about what happened when Abram (who later became Abraham) found out his nephew Lot had been taken captive.

Now when Abram heard that his brother was taken captive, he armed his three hundred and eighteen trained servants who were born in his own house, and went in pursuit as far as Dan. He divided his forces against them by night, and he and his servants attacked them and pursued them as far as Hobah, which is north of Damascas. So he brought back all the goods, and also brought back his brother Lot and his goods, as well as the women and the people.

Abraham took personally anything that happened to his nephew, Lot.

In a covenant, we have the mindset that the other person is a part of us and completes us. Of course we all are ultimately complete in Christ, but here on earth God has given us all different talents and strengths to help one another, particularly in marriage. Everything we do, say, and think should edify and build up our covenant partner in the same way we would personally want to be treated. We have all heard the "Golden Rule" of "Do unto others as you would want them to do to you." When both husband and wife take on this covenant partner mindset, submission will not be difficult because covenant partners know and trust that their partner is always looking out for their best interest.

SUBMISSION COMPARED TO OBEDIENCE

We once heard an amazing testimony about a man who was not living for God yet, but his wife was. He told her she couldn't go to church one evening when she was leaving to go to a church service. She announced to her husband, "I will submit to you in every area to do with our household and life, but I am going to church tonight because the Bible tells me to. You are my husband, but Jesus is my Lord." After she left that night, her husband locked the door so she could not get back in.

The next morning he went and opened the door to find her tightly huddled up against it trying to stay warm because it was so cold outside. She jumped up with enthusiasm, walked into the house and said, "What can I make you for breakfast this morning, dear?" This husband committed his life to the Lord shortly after this and went on to become a world-known evangelist. This wife may not have obeyed her husband's orders regarding not attending church, but she certainly had a submissive and loving heart!

What is true submission and how does it relate to obedience? When we look to Scripture for our definition, we will find submission includes having the right attitude, while obedience is simply an action. Quite often, a person obeys and submits at the same time, but this is not always the case. It is possible to obey, yet not submit, and it is also possible to have a submissive heart, yet not obey. Obedience without submission is like the little boy who was being loud in church one Sunday morning. Since the parents were not handling the situation, the pastor finally said in a loud voice, "Sonny, sit down and be quiet!" The little boy sat down and whispered, "I may be sitting down on the outside, but I'm standing up on the inside!"

There are four main areas the Bible admonishes us as adults to submit: to our government (Romans 13:1-7), within the body of Christ (1 Peter 5:5-6, Ephesians 5:21), the wife to her husband (Ephesians 5:22-24, Colossians 3:18-19), and man to Christ (1 Peter 3:7). We will mainly look at the last two mentioned.

But I want you to know that the head of every man is Christ, the head of woman is man, and the head of Christ is God (1 Corinthians 11:3).

God knew a man would be a quality leader in the home if he submits to Christ. In addition to Jesus' redemptive work for mankind that He did on the cross, His life was also set as an example to the husband of how to lead in the home. If a man ever wonders how to handle a situation or question that arises in his home, he needs only to look to Jesus and how He handled similar situations. Jesus always considered others' needs before his own. He always had a servant's heart. He consistently invested quality time with God, His authority, to get direction for Himself and those closest to Him. He was open and honest and gave freely of himself.

The Bible gives specific admonition and direction for husbands to follow in their role of being a leader who is pleasing to God.

Husbands, likewise, dwell with them with understanding, giving honor to the wife, as to the weaker vessel, and as being heirs together of the grace of life, that your prayers may not be hindered (1 Peter 3:7).

The word translated as *honor* here means "valuable, esteem to the highest degree, dignity, and precious" (Strong's #6092). Therefore, a husband is to treat his wife as being extremely valuable, esteem her to the highest degree, and treat her with dignity as being precious to him. When he makes a leadership decision, although the final decision should be in his hands, he should definitely give valuable consideration to her opinion on the subject at hand because the wife is often a confirmation to the husband. Listening to her input, especially when she feels very strong about an issue to do with your own household, is extremely important and may prevent serious mistakes.

Submission, as mentioned earlier, is ordained by God to keep unity and order within an organization or body. Ephesians 5:22-24 states,

> **Wives submit to your own husbands, as to the Lord. For the husband is head of the wife, as also Christ is the head of the church; and He is the Savior of the body. Therefore, just as the church is subject to Christ, so let the wives be to their own husbands in everything.**

How is the church subject to Christ? When we look to Him with respect and obey His Word with a willing heart and a good attitude. Do we see any place in the Bible where Christ *makes* the church submit or be subject to Him? No. In fact we find numerous instances of Him showing love even when His people were disobedient. Likewise, if a wife is not willing to submit, the husband should be patient. James 1:4 is great encouragement for husbands in this situation. *"But let patience have its perfect work, that you may be perfect and complete, lacking nothing."* Husbands, be encouraged and keep your faith in God. Believe for Him to work the situation out as you continue to keep a right heart toward your wife.

How can a wife submit to her husband as to the Lord, even if she does not agree with all of his decisions? Through daily reading the Word and making a conscious choice to be a doer of the Word. A wife who is a doer of the Word and focuses on walking in the fruits of the Spirit will find submission much easier than those who do not. As Galatians 6:22-25 shares,

But the fruit of the Spirit is love, joy, peace, longsuffering, kindness, goodness, faithfulness, gentleness, self-control. Against such there is no law. And those who are Christ's have crucified the flesh with its passions and desires. If we live in the Spirit, let us also walk in the Spirit.

We can conclude from this Scripture that when a wife chooses to walk in peace and kindness during an opportunity to submit to her husband, she will operate out of a Spirit of love rather than seeking her own desires. Love always does things God's way because God is love. True love is willing to give preference to and support another's way of doing things even when it is not easy. As Romans 12:10 states, *"Be kindly affectionate to one another with brotherly love, in honor giving preference to one another."*

WHAT IF A HUSBAND DOESN'T
SUBMIT TO CHRIST?

A wife may wonder, "Does God expect me to submit to my husband if he doesn't submit to Christ?" The answer is found in 1 Peter 3:1.

Wives, likewise, be submissive to your own husbands, that even if some do not obey the word, they, without a word, may be won by the conduct of their wives.

There are times when someone does not have to and even should not submit. One example of this is when it is someone who has no scriptural right to exercise authority over us. For example, there have been some people in times past who have taught that all women should submit to all men. This is definitely not true. Ephesians 5: 22 says, *"Wives, submit to your own husbands, as to the Lord."*

Also, we should always obey God's Word first and submit to others second. In Acts 5, Peter had been commanded by religious leaders not to preach in the name of Jesus anymore, but Peter chose to disobey and preach anyway. When confronted by the leaders he said in verse 29, *"We ought to obey God rather than men."* Peter was a man with a submissive heart, but he would not obey at the expense of disobedience to God.

Another submission issue women often question is, "Do I submit if my husband wants me to do things that go against God's Word, like watching porn?" Since the Word says we ought to obey God rather than men, this also includes obedience to his Word in the areas of lust and perversion. God desires his children who are married to have a great sex life together. God planned this as a blessing to His children within their marriage. However, God's blessing is not upon a married couple bringing worldly lust into their sex life through pornography, sex outside of marriage, or similar perversions. If one's spouse asks them to participate in or purchase things of this nature, it is against His Word, according to 1 John 2:15-16 which states,

Do not love the world or the things in the world. If anyone loves the world, the love of the Father is not in him. For all that is in the world—the lust of the flesh, the lust of the eyes, and the pride of life—is not of the Father but is of the world.

Sex within marriage is not of the world; it is of God because He created this union, and it pleases Him to know married couples are being fulfilled in this way. On the other hand, sex outside of marriage and pornography (the lust of the flesh and eyes) are Satan's plan to pervert what God intended to bless us. These are Satan's attempts to try to bring people, as well as their families, into bondage to him and into a life of pain, loss, and destruction if they fall into this trap.

HOW SUBMISSION CREATES EQUALITY

So how does submission create equality? Let us first look at Christ to find the answer. According to Scripture, Jesus was fully God, yet fully man. In His role here on earth as a man, he was tempted as we are tempted, yet without sin.

For we do not have a High Priest who cannot sympathize with our weaknesses, but was in all points tempted as we are, yet without sin (Hebrews 4:15).

Have you ever stopped to think about the fact that, as a man, He had to make the *choice to submit* to God the Father's perfect will for Him? This was demonstrated in various ways. For example when Satan came to tempt Him in the wilderness and showed Him all the earth's kingdoms, he said, *"All these things I will give you if you will fall down and worship me"* (Matthew 4:9). If Jesus had chosen to submit to Satan's will, which He did have the option of doing, He would have brought Himself into equality with Satan and the fallen realm of darkness.

Jesus did not have the same opportunity to repent that we have if we make a mistake. With Him it was all or nothing.

He had to be a spotless lamb in order to pay the price for the sins of a fallen world (see Hebrews 9:14). Since He did not give in to temptation, but instead chose to submit to God the Father's will, He made Himself equal with God. He expressed this in John 10:30 stating, *"I and My Father are one."* He made the choice through submission to God's will, to be one with the Father.

Another example of how submission creates equality comes from Romans 8:16-17. When we submit to God's plan of salvation and accept Jesus Christ as our personal Lord and Savior, the Scripture says we are then children of God, thereby making us, *"...heirs of God and joint heirs with Christ..."* (Romans 8:17). Therefore, through submission to God's will, which is His plan of salvation through Jesus Christ, we receive equality as joint heirs with Christ.

In most examples, the one submitting brings themselves into equality with the one they are submitting to. There is one opposite Scriptural scenario, which is the case of a believing wife with her husband. Although the husband is still to have the role as head of the home in God's eyes even if he does not submit to Christ, the wife is actually at a higher place spiritually than the husband if she is in Christ and the husband is not.

We read earlier in 1 Peter 3:1 the instruction to Christian wives married to unbelievers. It said to submit even if the husband does not follow the Word, that he might be won to the Lord through the respectful and pure conduct of his wife. It goes on in verse four to state that a wife should adorn herself with, *"...the incorruptible beauty of a gentle and quiet spirit, which is very precious in the sight of God."* In this case, the wife's Christ-like example of submission helps the husband come into equality with his wife by being born again through Christ and becoming equal as an heir of God with her!

We have had numerous women testify to us of what a wonderful experience this is to have shown their husband honor, respect, and submission, even when the husband did not act deserving of it, then see him brought into a close relationship with Christ because of the wife's heart toward him.

WHY DOES A HUSBAND NEED RESPECT?

Have you noticed that in the much acclaimed love chapter of Ephesians 5, it never makes comment of the husband needing love? It says the husband is to see to it that he loves his wife, but it says the wife is to see to it that she respects her husband. Respect means "to reverence" and "to be in awe of" (Strong's #5399). Why is respect so important, particularly to a man? It is important for many reasons, but one of the main reasons is that without respect, he cannot operate efficiently in the role he is called to as head of the home.

If the wife does not give her husband respect, this means she is also not honoring or trusting the decisions he makes and, therefore, is disregarding his God-ordained position in the home. In God's eyes, if a wife responds to her husband the same as she would if speaking to her other family members or friends, then she is not holding him in reverence or high regard. She is not esteeming him as worthy of greater honor than others, but rather treating him, his opinions, and his decisions as common. When a wife does not show respect to her husband as the head of her home, she in many ways makes him ineffective, in his role as head.

What are some ways wives show honor or lack of it? One example is the wife who would like a new car. If a husband responds by saying he doesn't think she needs a new car, the wife has several choices. First, she could go out and buy it anyway if she personally has the financial means to do so. This would be extremely dishonoring to her husband. Secondly, she could think to herself, "Well, I just need to be persistent and get him used to the idea." This is called nagging even if it is done politely, and is also dishonoring to a husband. Third, she could have initially brought the request in a way that would help him adequately understand her reason for wanting a new car.

Men often relate better to a word picture (just as Jesus used parables) than a plain request without any reasoning behind it. Then, if the husband was not in agreement after this kind of request was fully explained and understandable, the wife can say, "Honey, I trust God directs you as the leader of our home so, as much as I would like a new car right now,

I will respect what you say because I know you love me and always have my best interest in mind." Then the wife can just bring the need to the Lord in prayer and look to Him to supply all of her needs according to His riches in glory (see Philippians 4:19).

Submission and respect in marriage are much like a submarine in its proper environment of water. When the submarine is submerged, the captain can maneuver the submarine however is needed to be effective. The ship can be steered effectively, it can detect much with its radar, and it can even launch missiles at the enemy when needed. When a submarine is out of water, however, it can't perform properly. The instruments may move, but in most areas, the submarine is ineffective without water. Likewise, when a wife chooses not to submit and thereby, not to respect her husband, the couple often sits like a submarine out of water. The husband and his family may be able to do a few small things God has called them to, but it is nowhere near what they could do if his wife were in submission and agreement with him.

When a husband lives in an environment of consistent respect from his wife, he is able to guide their ship peacefully and with little difficulty because there is great power in unity. He sees and knows that his wife trusts him and believes in his decision-making ability. Her respect for him even increases his determination to make quality decisions to benefit her and the family.

Many women do not realize that respect is also what often creates or diminishes attraction in a relationship for a male. When a man feels respected by his wife, he typically feels more attracted to her and will make a greater effort to be an excellent husband. Adversely, if he frequently feels disrespected by his wife, his attraction may eventually start to wane. For this reason, a wife who values her marriage and desires to please God will make every effort to respect and honor her husband.

In one of my former places of employment, there was a young man I worked with who happened to mention in conversation that his parents were divorced. I asked him if they were both saved at the time of their divorce. He said yes. So I inquired more, telling him that my husband and I do marriage ministry and like to find out the reasons why Christians have been divorced to help us in our teaching. He looked surprised at the thought and said he really didn't know why they had divorced. He remembered at the time of their marriage difficulties that his mom was always saying how irresponsible his dad was. He frequently heard her tell his dad that he didn't make enough money to take care of the family and he wouldn't help around the house.

I then inquired, "Is your dad really lazy?" He said, "Well, no, actually he isn't. He worked his way to the top of the company he's been with many years and is now second in command to the owner, who is a very old woman and a kind, grandmother type figure. She is always telling him, as well as us kids when we see her, how wonderful our dad is and that she thinks he is such a hard worker." I said, "Oh, I see why they divorced. Your mom didn't respect him with her words to his face or in front of you kids, so she ate the fruit of her lips. Her husband continued to disappoint her and their marriage even failed. On the other hand, the owner of the company voiced her respect and honor towards him with her words and she ate the fruit of her lips, getting an excellent employee who would do anything he could to please her!" He looked at me so surprised and said, "Wow! You are right! I never realized that before, but it is true. My dad remarried and his second wife is very respectful and approving of him, and he is a great husband to her."

In a situation like this, of course, a person can't put all of the blame on the wife for the failure of the marriage because his actions certainly played a part in their problems. It illustrates an excellent point though. The husband was willing to do for one woman, what he was not willing to do for the other, all because of the respect issue. One woman created an environment that focused on and affirmed failure, and that is exactly what she received. The other woman provided an environment of respect and positive affirmation, and through her response brought inevitable success!

AMY: MORE BENEFTIS OF SUBMISSION

Why is submission to the God-chosen and God-ordained leader a good thing? In Hebrews 13:17 we read,

Obey those who rule over you, and be submissive, for they watch out for your souls, as those who must give account. Let them do so with joy and not with grief, for that would be unprofitable for you.

This Scripture is referring to all those who rule over us. It could mean leaders at work, husbands, parents of young children, or numerous other roles. If disobedience to those in authority is "unprofitable," then we can infer that obedience and submission will be profitable to us.

In other words, if we choose to set ourselves in agreement with their decisions and do it with joy, even if it is not something we initially desire, God will see to it that, in the end, we gain benefit from submission! I don't know about you, but I want to have benefit and gain from the direction of my husband. I also want to make his life easy, not only because I love him, but also because I know one day I will stand before God and be held accountable for whether I willingly followed the leader of my home or if he had to deal with the challenges of a difficult and obstinate wife.

Proverbs 12:4 states, *"An excellent wife is the crown of her husband, but she who causes shame is like rotten- ness in his bones."* When a wife chooses to walk in unity with her husband, she is choosing to be a crown to him. The original meaning of the Hebrew word translated as "crown" in this passage means to encircle (for attack or protection). In this case the writer of Proverbs was obviously using it to mean to encircle for protection (Strong's, #5849). The same Hebrew word used for crown in Proverbs 12:4 is also used in Proverbs 4:9 which tells us that wisdom also brings a crown of glory on one's head.

Therefore, an excellent wife will do everything she can to be a source of Godly wisdom to her husband. She will do her best to help him, as well as support his choices and decisions as long as they don't make her go against God's Word. This means she will not manipulate or nag, but rather she will pray for him and share her thoughts with him on a matter after she has prayed over it. It is important for a wife to remember that females can be very persuasive at times. Therefore, she should be all the more watchful not to push her husband into jumping ahead of God's plan. It is vital to remember that if God has made us a promise in His Word or given us direction through His Holy Spirit, we are to wait on His timing and trust our husband to be led of the Lord.

Why else is it profitable to submit with a willing heart? The enemy wants to do everything he can to keep a married couple out of unity and agreement because he knows that when they are in agreement following God, he cannot get his foot in the door. One main reason a wife often does not want to submit is for self-seeking reasons, because she does not see the decision her husband wants to make as a benefit for herself. If the wife refuses to submit, her self-seeking can open the door in her life to the enemy according to James 3:16 which states, "*For where envy and self-seeking exist, confusion and every evil thing are there.*"

I remember one time when Shaun believed we should give a large financial gift to a certain ministry. It was at a time in our life when we knew we had extra financial needs arising within a few months. When he initially shared this with me and asked if I was in agreement with him, I said no. We had given larger offerings to ministries than this before, and at very difficult times. However I was not investing as much time in the Word at this point in my life, and therefore I was putting my trust in money rather than God. The next day he discussed it with me again, asking me to trust that God is faithful and we would reap what we sowed financially, just as a farmer plants seeds in the ground and expects to receive the harvest of a crop.

He waited to give the offering because he believes as a leader that we should both be in agreement when we sow a large financial gift. He also wanted me to have a cheerful heart in giving. I went to God and asked Him to put some sense into Shaun on this issue, but instead God started working on my heart to knock some spiritual sense back into me. Within two days the Lord had helped me to have a submissive heart and give cheerfully. I told Shaun I was in agreement with him and we sent the money. Shortly after sending the money, without telling anyone our needs that were coming up, three people gave us a total of the exact amount we needed at the time, which was three times more than we had sent to that ministry.

SHAUN AND AMY: BECOMING WILLING

It is easy to submit to leaders when we are in agreement with them, but the true test of submission comes when the going gets tough and we have to do something we do not want to do. When Jesus was praying in the garden at Gethsemane, He said, *"O My Father, if it is possible, let this cup pass from Me; nevertheless, not as I will, but as You will"* (Matthew 26:39). Jesus knew what He was about to face and He even sweat drops of blood over it the Bible says.

As we read the words He prayed to the Father in the garden, we see that He kept going to the Lord for strength until His heart became submissive to the Father's will. The first time Jesus states outright that as a man, it was not His desire or will to suffer this. Yet the more He prayed in the garden, and was open to be made willing, He received the mindset of God the Father's agape love to die to save the people. This is shown through His change in words from the first prayer to the second and third prayer. First He said,

"...not as I will, but as you will" (Matthew 26:39). Then the next two prayers He says, *"Oh My Father, if this cup cannot pass away from Me unless I drink it, Your will be done"* (Matthew 26:42). The second and third times He no longer said it was not His will because through prayer, Jesus had allowed the heart of the Father to come in and make Him willing. As a result, you and I have been blessed with eternal life with Jesus when we ask Him into our heart.

One of our favorite submission stories about a person becoming willing was from an associate pastor. His senior pastor made a decision that he did not like or want to follow. When he went to the Lord about it, he said the Lord spoke clearly to his heart saying, "Sometimes I specifically do not tell you what I am directing your leader to do, just to see if you willingly submit to his authority and follow him as he follows Christ." This is a good lesson for all of us to remember.

SUBMITTING TO HIS MASTER PLAN

Matthew 6:33 says that if we put God and His righteousness first place in our lives, everything else will be added unto us. Psalm 37:4 says *"Delight yourself also in the Lord and He shall give you the desires of your heart."* If you do not have all of the desires of your heart right now, choose to be joyful and thank God for those things you do have. Trust that as you serve God, which includes being submissive to those He has placed over you, you will come to the place where you lack nothing (see James 1:4). God is faithful to His Word and will surely reward you for diligently seeking Him and following His way of doing things.

As we follow Christ's example of submission, we will find ourselves moving closer toward the fulfillment of His master plan for our life. This plan for our life includes peace in our home and workplace. When we, the Body of Christ, submit to His perfect plan of submission and respect, then peace is attained. He created this plan for us to follow, so we would know how to keep the enemy out and how to keep love in at all times. Godly submission and respect for the leader of our family causes us to become a great success and causes God's work to be completed in the earth.

Godly Submission

1. Proper submission is intended to bring peace and blessing.
2. Submission is a heart issue, not just an obedience issue.
3. We should not disobey God and His Word in order to submit.
4. When we joyfully submit to our husband, it will be profitable for us.

Chapter 8

Successful Leadership in the Home

...For if a man does not know how to rule his own house, how will he take care of the church of God (1 Timothy 3:5)?

Aphrase often used in business circles is "The speed of the leader is the speed of the gang." This saying characterizes the day in which we live. It seems everything is about speed. How fast can we get it done? How fast can we get there? How fast can this machine run? Fast is great! But when it comes to great leaders, God is not looking for someone who will just focus on getting the job done fast. He is looking for people who will get the job done with excellence.

God set high standards on leadership positions in His church. Why? Because He wants believers to have excellent role models in order to become the best leaders in the world.

He knows that what is in the head will flow into the body, and He wants His body taking dominion here on the earth!

In the day we live, books on leadership in the workplace abound. People have learned how to achieve promotion, how to lead their companies, and how to make it to the top of their profession. Yet at the same time of great leaders abounding in the earth, we have seen marriages fail and families fall apart at alarming rates! What is the answer to this dilemma? We believe the answer begins with a study of leadership in the home. According to 1 Timothy 3:5, striving to achieve a leadership position before it has been achieved in the home, is like the old adage of putting the cart before the horse. God knows that whether in the ministry or the workplace, the joys of success achieved are much greater when a person has a peaceful environment to come home to and enjoy the fruit of their labor.

Architects tell us that the taller they plan to build a building, the deeper they plan and place the foundational footings under the ground in order to support the building to keep it from tipping over. This is a perfect illustration of why God desires that believers have strong marriages and families. He knows that the deeper a marriage and family is rooted in God's love and unity, the higher that family can build and the more dominion they can take in the earth to achieve greatness for God.

SHAUN: LOVING CHRIST FIRST

The most basic requirement to be a successful leader in our home is having our priorities in order. We know this means first and foremost, loving God and seeking to know Him with all of our heart. I remember, in the early years of our marriage, having to get this area in proper place in my own life. Before marriage, I would wake up in the morning by myself and enjoy time with the Lord before going to work or college. After marriage, I noticed God started to give me new opportunities to see whether or not I was still keeping Him first place in my life. I believe these opportunities were more for me to see where my heart was, than for Him to see, because He already knew.

Often these opportunities to put God first place came in the middle of the night. I remember one cold winter night the first year we were married. We were living in Minnesota, and it was well below freezing outside. It was twelve o'clock in the morning and I woke up to what sounded like knocking on our bedroom window. When I was fully awake, I didn't hear it anymore, but I went and looked out our second-story window anyway. Nothing was outside. I started to go back to bed when I clearly sensed the Lord saying to me, "I would like to have some time with you." I thought, "Oh, Lord, it's cold in here. I'm tired and I just want to go back to bed. I'll have time with you in the morning." I crawled back into bed and snuggled up with Amy and went to sleep again.

A half hour later I awoke to the same sound of knocking on the window. I got up and looked out again and nothing was out there that would make that kind of noise. Again I had a prompting in my heart from the Lord nudging me, "I want to have time with you." Again I said, "God, it's cold in here and I'm tired." I went back to sleep again.

This happened a third time that night and I'm embarrassed to say, I did the same thing again. However, this time when I lay back down, Amy sat straight up in bed completely asleep and said with authority, "The Apostle John would have gone outside in 60 below zero weather to wake himself up, if the Lord wanted to have time with him!" Then she lay back down and kept sleeping. When I asked Amy the next morning if she remembered saying anything to me in the night she said no, she didn't remember a thing!

I had been studying about John being the "apostle of love" before this experience and had prayed that God would help me to become more like he was. I learned a valuable lesson about putting God first place in my life, and now God knows He can wake me up whenever He desires and I will get up to have time with Him. Placing Him first place may not always seem like the easiest thing to do at the time, but it always proves to be the most beneficial.

Occasionally, people are concerned about placing God first in their life, thinking this would require setting aside their vocation in order to seek God, as though it were a full-time job, and read their Bible 50 hours a week. However, the truth is, God is a very reasonable God. He never asks for more than we can give. Placing God first simply means we invest time with Him at the start of each day by reading the Word and having fellowship with Him. This will then help us keep a tender and yielded heart toward Him throughout the day as we go about our work. We treat Him as an ever-present friend who has all the answers and is always at our side.

The Word admonishes us that we are to put Him first place, before our family. A person cannot be a truly effective leader that brings about eternal change for God's kingdom without doing so. In Luke 14:26 we read,

If anyone comes to Me and does not hate his father and mother, wife and children, brothers and sisters, yes, and his own life also, he cannot be My disciple.

It is important to understand with this Scripture that the word the English translators used as "hate" is actually the Greek word "miseo", which can mean either "to detest" or "to love less" (Strong's #3404). Since God is a God of love, in this case it means "to love less." So this Scripture is really saying that anyone who does not love Jesus more than he loves his father, mother, wife, children, brothers, sisters, and his own life, is not worthy to be called His disciple.

LOVING FAMILY SECOND

When we consistently maintain God as first place in our life, we are then prepared to be the quality spouse, parent, or any other leader God has called us to be. When He is truly first place in our life, our words and actions will show on a consistent basis the fruits of the Spirit, which are *"...love, joy, peace, longsuffering, kindness, goodness, faithfulness, gentleness, and self-control"* (Galatians 5:22). With these operating through us, we are then able to have healthy relationships in our home, particularly with our children and spouse.

In order to be a Christ-like leader in the home and keep family in proper priority, certain standards are necessary. These standards include building a strong spiritual foundation as a family, as well as honoring each other and having quality time together. In addition to having a great church to attend together, a strong spiritual foundation can be built through prayer together within the marriage and with the children.

When God is given an open door to a family through unified prayer and spiritual fellowship together, He is able to freely direct the path of the family. As Proverbs 3:6 states, *"In all your ways acknowledge Him, and He shall direct your paths."* Praying with our spouse and children is an excellent way of showing them that we love them so much that we want to build a spiritual bond with them, which is the most important bond of all.

Honor is also essential to maintaining a healthy emotional relationship with our family. To dishonor someone means to treat him or her as common. Therefore, to honor someone is to place great value on them. This is often displayed through our words and actions.

One of our favorite marriage teachers says that when he sees his wife or children he sometimes says something like, "Oh, my goodness! I can hardly believe I get to live in the same house with someone so wonderful!" Was it easy for this man to learn to value his family members? Probably not. He grew up in a home where anger, arguments, and lack of respect were a regular occurrence. After growing up in a very unhealthy and dishonoring home, he chose to stop the cycle of verbal abuse and do things God's way with his family.

Quality time together is essential to building a healthy physical bond with each other as a family. This can include anything a family likes to do, without interruptions or distractions from outside sources. Some of our favorite times together are camping, going for a picnic at a lake, hiking in the woods, going to a resort for a weekend, all without the cell phone.

Some people need more quality time together than others, so families need to determine the amount of time they need themselves. We personally believe that if possible, it is good for a family to have quality time at least once a week. We have met successful families who do this only once a month. However, these families do maintain a very strong spiritual and emotional bond through prayer and honor consistently throughout the month.

PURSUIT OF CAREER THIRD

Many times we meet people who put their career first in life. We believe that if people understood how beneficial it is to have God and family before their career, they would quickly get this in proper order. We have seen ministers and business people neglect giving their relationship with God or their relationship with their family adequate attention, and then wonder why God has allowed their children to rebel or their wife or husband to run off with someone. The truth is, God didn't allow it, but rather they did. Although work and ministry is good and necessary, it cannot take the place of a personal relationship with God each day. God also gives clear instruction in 1 Timothy 3:5 that a man is supposed to rule his own house well even before taking care of the church. The word translated as *rule* in the Greek here also means to "maintain" (Strong's #4291). Therefore, this is telling us if a man is not maintaining his family, he is not adequately suited to take care of the church either. Ministers and businesspeople alike are wise to evaluate the condition of their family on a regular basis and make necessary adjustments to bring love, quality time together, and order into their home.

It is disappointing to see men or women going into ministry who think that ministry is supposed to be a twenty-four hour, seven-day a week job and their family is just going to have to learn to deal with never seeing them anymore. They would be better off not marrying than to give the Word of God a black eye through their misunderstanding of God's priorities. Certainly God does not want us to neglect our calling in life, but He does expect us to maintain balance and order.

We know a number of very large ministries who place an emphasis on family life and marriage not being neglected at the expense of ministering. This scriptural belief was worded well by one well-known senior pastor of 20 years from a several-thousand-member church near us. He says that his first responsibility in being a minister to people is to minister to his own family! He also does not allow any of his associate ministers to work over 50 hours a week because he wants them to have a family life and be an example to other believers in the church. Interestingly, we have noticed that the ministries with these Scriptural priorities also tend to be the ones who do well financially and don't beg people for money.

Another leadership topic we encounter is women with wonderful talents and leadership abilities that sometimes wonder whether God is calling them to work outside the home or not. Based on the Word of God, the wife is first called to be a helper to the husband. Genesis 2:18 states,

And the Lord God said, 'It is not good that man should be alone; I will make him a helper comparable to him.'

God is a peace-giving God, which is why He set certain things in place in the home to bring about a peaceful atmosphere. Therefore, one of the main roles of the calling to be a helper includes helping create an atmosphere of peace in the home. Secondly, a wife may be called to work in a position outside the home, as long as it doesn't conflict with keeping peace in the home.

The virtuous wife described in Proverbs 31 was excellent at keeping peace and order in her home, and she was a great businesswoman and investor. If peace can be maintained in the home and the husband is in agreement with the wife working outside the home, then a wife should pursue this if she feels led by God to do so. When the husband is in agreement, he should then be willing to support the wife when needed, such as helping with the kids or other duties necessary to help her. In making career choices it is important for both a husband and wife to remember that God is pleased when families maintain the priority of having a peaceful home and raising Christ-like children.

SHAUN: LEADING BY EXAMPLE

...But whoever desires to become great among you, let him be your servant...just as the Son of Man did not come to be served, but to serve... (Matthew 20:26, 28).

As believers, we would certainly all agree that Jesus is the ultimate example of leadership. Throughout his life on earth He gave us many examples of how effective leadership works, so we will look at a few of His characteristics in order to learn from His ways. First, Jesus led with a servant's heart and specifically taught His followers how they were to conduct themselves in order to be Christ-like leaders. He said that gentile leaders lord it over those they lead and exercise their authority over them. In other words, the gentile leaders were prideful about their leadership roles and forced others into submission. Then Jesus advised, *"Yet it shall not be so among you; but whoever desires to become great among you, let him be your servant"* (Matthew 20:26). He then went on to use Himself as an example stating, *"...just as the Son of Man did not come to be served, but to serve, and to give His life a ransom for many"* (Matthew 20:28).

I remember once in our early years, Amy had received news that her great-uncle, who was like a grandfather to her, was about to pass on. Although he was very old and ready to go, Amy was sad about it. I tried to cheer her up in several ways, which didn't seem to help. Finally, I prayed and asked God what I could do to help make this easier on her, which I should have done in the beginning.

After praying, a very clear thought dropped in my heart, which was to wash her feet. I almost laughed out loud because the thought seemed so ridiculous to me at the time. I responded back and said, "God, she would laugh at me if I did that. I know Jesus washed His disciples feet, but that was many years ago. People don't do things like that anymore. Can you give me another idea?" Again I just had the clear thought to wash her feet. So finally I went and got a towel and a bucket filled with soap and water, went over to where she was sitting and began to wash her feet. She lifted her head and looked at me. Then I saw the tears stop and a big smile come to her face. She said, "Shaun, I love you."

When this happened I realized that Jesus' example of being a servant leader is just as important today as it was when He walked the earth. Whether it is washing someone's feet or just getting them a glass of water, I always remember my lesson from God: true love serves. My own human ideas failed to help my wife, but God knew what she needed all along. Whether it is with our spouse or our children, it is comforting to know that God always knows and is willing to give us the right answer.

Another example Jesus gave us was to use reward motivation when possible. God promises to reward us when we diligently seek Him. He even reminds us in Revelation 22:12

that we will be rewarded according to our works here on earth. Two forces typically motivate people: consequences or reward, loss or gain. When training children, it is certainly necessary at times to use discipline as a consequence of disobedience, just as the book of Proverbs admonishes. Sometimes, however, chronic disobedience in young and old may simply be from a lack of positive motivation to do the right thing. People of all ages tend to respond very well to motivation through rewards and praise. Certainly there were times when Jesus rebuked and corrected people. However, He often gave reward incentives such as telling them that in His Father's house are many mansions and He was going to prepare one for them.

We remember one such leader who used reward motivation. He was a girls' track coach and a wonderful Christian man. He instructed and trained the girls just as any good coach, but there was one thing that set him apart from other leaders. He looked for ways that he could be a gift to the girls on his team and show appreciation. He would express thankfulness for their hard work in practice, and he would also do little things to show appreciation, such as bringing to a track meet a cooler filled with roses and giving one to each of his team members after the meet.

AMY: APPRECIATIVE LEADERSHIP

A leader can demonstrate one of two mindsets to his or her followers. They can either act like those following them should be thankful to have such a great leader, or they can humbly demonstrate that they are honored to be able to lead such exceptional and wonderful people. I often hear Shaun, as he is kissing our children goodnight, say things like, "I love you and I'm so thankful to get to be your daddy!" or "Thank you for being so good today. You make it so fun to be a dad." Our kids then get the biggest smile and say, "You're welcome, daddy!"

Jesus also demonstrated great leadership by being truthful. Jesus even said in John 14:6, *"I am the way, the truth, and the life."* If we tell an untruth, we separate ourselves from Him because He is truth and we then open the door to let failure in. If God can trust us with the small, He can trust us with the large. Also, if we do make a mistake as a leader, we can go to those who follow us and be an example to them of a humble heart.

I like to use opportunities for honesty to be an example to our children. I once went through a drive up restaurant. After getting part way home I noticed the person had given me a dollar extra in change. When I got home, I called and let them know they had given me a dollar too much. I was speaking with the manager and he told me, "You don't need to bring the dollar back, but I would like to buy you and your family dinner on us for being so honest. That's rare." It may be rare in the world, but God's plan is for it to be the standard among believers!

AMY: AFFIRMING THOSE WE LEAD

One of our personal favorites of Jesus' leadership qualities was that He affirmed those under His authority. He said to His disciples in the upper room, those who were closest to Him,

No longer do I call you servants, for a servant does not know what his master is doing, but I have called you friends, for all things that I heard from My Father I have made known to you. You did not choose Me, but I chose you and appointed you that you should go and bear fruit, and that your fruit should remain, that whatever you ask the Father in My name He may give you (John 15:15-16).

What a statement! He affirmed them by calling them friends and emphasizing that He chose them. He then spoke blessing over them, telling them that He chose them for a valuable purpose and calling. He believed with all of His heart that they would succeed in this calling. He then gave them a promise saying that whatever they asked God for in

His name, they would receive it! The exciting thing for us as believers is, He was also speaking this over you and me! Jesus believed in His disciples, and He believes in us just as much today because we are also His disciples called to do His will in the earth.

What profound value this example of Christ has to bring God's love and unity into our homes today! Friend, whoever you lead, one of the most basic, yet important, keys to guiding them to become a success in life is to affirm that you are thankful they are in your life. Then let them know you believe in them, you believe in their future, and you are committed to them. When spouses do this with each other and parents do this with children consistently in their home, it completely transforms a family.

I remember once as a teenager telling my mother about someone who had just found out that they were adopted. The person's parents evidently didn't know how to tell him, so they never did, until one day when he was a teenager and he found out another way. When I shared this with my mom, she made the comment that as a parent adoption is not any different than having a baby born to you, so she wished people would just explain this to their kids when they were little.

She then told me a story about one of my siblings who is adopted. She said that when very young, she simply said, "There are three ways that someone can become part of a family. First, you can choose a spouse and marry into a family. That is how I became a part of our family. I chose your Dad and he chose me, and we became a family. Second, you can be born into a family. That means a mom has a baby grow in her tummy and after nine months of being in the mom's tummy the baby comes out. Sometimes if a mom can't take care of her baby, she will let a couple adopt the baby because she wants the baby to have a wonderful life with a mom and a dad. That is the third way you can become a part of a family is to be adopted into a family. That means that a mom and dad want to have a child to love of their very own, so they go and choose the baby that they want to be part of their family. That is how you became part of our family. Daddy and I chose you because we wanted you to be part of our family so much, just like Daddy and I chose each other!"

I was amazed at the wisdom in her explaining it this way. I used to work with a woman who explained this in a similar way to her daughter who had been adopted. She said her daughter would come to her every few months and say, "Mommy, tell me the story again about how you and Daddy chose me!" It is important to let children know the truth at a young age so that the emphasis can be placed on the important information. They are chosen, loved, and wanted in the position they have in the family! That is essentially what Jesus was saying to His disciples. I love you! I wanted you as my disciples! I believe in you! I am confident you are going to be a success even after I am gone!

This is pretty amazing when you consider the disciples He had chosen. They didn't come from any special background, and they didn't have a theology degree. There was nothing extraordinary about them except that they were willing to be vessels for God to work through. For this reason, they did mighty things to advance God's kingdom here on earth. Jesus seemed to receive great joy over making something great out of people society considered common. As we have heard our pastor say, "God is a champion at making a somebody out of a nobody."

AMY: AFFIRMING OUR FAMILY

We have this same ability Jesus operated in within our own home. We can make a difference to those closest to us by believing in them, no matter what. Showing confidence in someone does amazing things. Shaun often says that when we believe enough in someone's success, they will eventually become a success. We can change the whole environment in our home just by showing approval and confidence in our family members!

It is rewarding to see someone who was doing average or below average in life with no real goals for their future suddenly experience someone who believes in them. It typically changes everything! Most people like to live up to their leaders' or loved ones' expectations when they are spoken to with love and belief. Children and adults standards are raised when they know someone has positive expectancy over them. Hearing things like:

You can do it! I know you can!
I believe in you! You are going to do great!
Way to go! You did a great job!
I am so pleased with you!
Thank you for doing your best!

I remember once in fifth grade when I had gotten an F on a social studies test. I normally earned A's and B's so it was probably a big surprise for my mom and dad when I came home with this news. I had misunderstood what chapter I was to study, so I was not prepared for the test I took. I still remember my mom, who is one of the most encouraging people I know, saying to me, "All that matters to me, honey, is that you did your best. I will always be pleased with you as long as you try. Don't feel bad about it. You are smart and you'll bring your grade back up next time." I went from having a feeling of condemnation to having joy because I knew I was accepted and loved. I was reminded that she believed in me and in my future. She helped me get things back in perspective. My life wasn't over because of an F on a test!

Friend, just as my mom believed in me and let me know it, God believes in you too! He has let us know it all through His Word. Jesus voiced His confidence and approval to His disciples, but He was also saying this to you and me. You are special to Him! He equipped you with everything you need to be a success in life, not only in your profession, but also as a spouse and parent. 2 Corinthians 9:8 tells us,

And God is able to make all grace abound toward you, that you, always having all sufficiency in all things, may have an abundance for every good work.

This verse is specifically referring to those who cheerfully give money to God's work here on the earth. It implies that when money is given to God's kingdom, God's grace will see to it that all of our needs will be met and that we have even more to give. This also can apply to anything we give cheerfully to benefit His kingdom and further His Gospel here on earth. When we give our spouse and children praise, affirmation, and encouragement, we are showing them a demonstration of how loving our Father in heaven is. When those we live with experience God's goodness manifested through us, it will draw their hearts into a greater desire to know Him and His love more deeply. When we cheerfully give praise to others, we make ourselves able to experience more of the good God has planned for us. Another way of saying this is, the more love and approval we give to others, the more joy we will experience ourselves!

God's grace manifested in us can and will give us the ability and knowledge to be an encourager to our family and to others we lead. Being an encourager is not a personality type, but rather it is a choice. Even if you have not been one to verbalize encouragement and approval to those around you, know that God can help you do this! Although it had not been Shaun's "personality" to be an encourager of others when he was young, as an adult he saw the value in this behavior and determined to learn this good quality. With God's help he trained himself to do this and is now an excellent encourager to others. If you would like to grow in this area, you can even pray this right now:

Father, I ask You to help me see the best in my family and those I lead. Please help me to voice approval of them and belief in them on a daily basis. I pray that they will experience my love and Your love through me each day in a tangible way. In Jesus name, amen.

Godly Leadership
1. Remember our leadership first begins in the home.
2. Keep your priorities in order: God, family, career.
3. Be a cheerful servant to those you lead.
4. Willingly lavish praise on those you lead.

Chapter 9

Absence in the Heart Draws the Family Apart

Do not deprive one another except with consent for a time, that you may give yourselves to fasting and prayer; and come together again so that Satan does not tempt you because of your lack of self-control (1 Corinthians 7:5).

"I'd give it all up! The awards I have achieved and wealth I have earned, I'd give it all up just to have my marriage and family back." For those of us in marriage ministry, it is not uncommon to hear these words in the day we live, especially from those who have seemed to be more married to their work than they are to their spouse. Someone realizes too late that there were things they could have or should have done differently on their quest to success. Their spouse seemed to be happy, and they thought they were doing a decent job as a spouse. What happened?

Most people have heard the old saying, "Absence makes the heart grow fonder." To any person who believes this saying, we would like to ask the question, "Do you believe absence from the Lord in prayer and Bible reading draws you closer to Him?" Of course you would say no, and so it is with marriage.

The more time we invest with our spouse in mutually fulfilling activities and meaningful time together, the better we will understand and grow close to each other. Likewise, the more time we spend apart from our spouse, the more distance we will have in our relationship with each other. Certainly there may be occasions when it is impossible to avoid separation, such as when a spouse is sent for military duty. However, whenever separation can be avoided, it should be.

SHAUN AND AMY: UNITY IN MARRIAGE

Rather than learning to mold two lives together in unity as God intended, some couples want to maintain completely separate identities and continue after marriage with different friends, separate activities, and sometimes even separate vacations. They make little to no effort to unify their lives into one. God, however, has a plan for unity in marriage. Building unity requires a couple growing in intimacy with each other on a consistent basis, similar to how Christ desires to be in intimate relationship with His church. Just as spiritual intimacy between a person and God is achieved through making regular, quality time with God, also spiritual, emotional, and physical intimacy in marriage is achieved through quality time regularly invested with our spouse.

Hosea 4:6 states, *"My people are destroyed for lack of knowledge."* This Scripture was referring to people who had rejected the knowledge of God. However, the principle of this is true no matter what the reason. Lack of knowledge will eventually bring destruction. Satan knows that if he can keep believers separated from their relationship with the Lord through lack of prayer, Bible study, and fellowship with other believers, they will lack knowledge of God's Word and God's ways. Then Satan will have a greater opportunity to deceive and destroy them. If he can separate believers from the Word and proper teaching, they will lack knowledge of their covenant rights in the Lord and will be less effective for God. This also is true of marriage. Since the marriage union represents Christ and the church, Satan will do everything he can to convince a couple that regular time spent apart has no effect on their relationship, which will in turn cause the marriage to be less effective for God's kingdom.

STAYING CONNECTED WHEN SEPARATED BY DISTANCE

We know of a pastor who was at a ministers' conference and had a hotel room by himself. Later in the evening, he went to the hotel's restaurant for a late night snack, and the waitress began flirting with him. He left the restaurant quickly, returned to his room, and called his wife. He told her what had happened and said he felt very tempted and was fighting these feelings by reading the Word. He also wanted her to know so she could pray for him.

This pastor did the right thing in telling his wife and was making an effort to stay spiritually and emotionally connected with his wife even though they were apart. Sadly however, his wife did the wrong thing in her response. She said, "Why are you telling me this? Do you think I want to hear about you being attracted to another woman?" This wife was completely ignorant or possibly in denial of the temptations that are in the world that Christians also encounter. She wanted to stick her head in the sand instead of thanking God she had a husband who was honest with her and was humble enough to share his struggle and ask for her help.

If our spouse comes to us for help with sexual temptation, rather than getting offended, hurt, or feeling mistrust, we should be honored that they truly treat us as their best friend, and look to us for help in overcoming the obstacle. We should embrace them warmly, pray for them, encourage them, and affirm our physical relationship with them. Our spouse being honest and asking for help should increase our trust for them because they are not keeping anything hidden, and therefore, they are not giving the enemy any place in the marriage.

If a pastor at a ministers' conference can struggle with sexual temptations, should we think our husband or wife who is on a trip (or home during a spouse's trip) is exempt from temptations? 1 Corinthians 7:5 says,

Do not deprive one another except with consent for a time, that you may give yourselves to fasting and prayer; and come together again so that Satan does not tempt you because of your lack of self-control.

God desires for us to maintain a healthy physical relationship with our spouse and not neglect this area. If you or your spouse do take business trips that are currently unavoidable, it is wise to invest time praying and believing for you to both stay strong spiritually, emotionally, and physically.

TRAVEL TOGETHER

Paul makes an interesting statement in 1 Corinthians 9:5. *"Do we have no right to take along a believing wife, as do also the other apostles, the brothers of the Lord, and Cephas?"* Many people pass over this Scripture, but we would encourage believers to take a closer look at this. It is saying that the other apostles, the brothers of the Lord, and Cephas had the right, and obviously exercised it, to take along a believing wife when they traveled. Paul would not have known they had the right to, if they were not doing so.

As we mentioned before, there may be times when a couple has to travel without their spouse. However, we encourage couples to pray that God would make a way for them to start traveling as a family if travel will continue to be necessary for their line of work.

If a husband's relationship to a wife is truly a representation of Christ's relationship to the church as Ephesians 5 illustrates it should be, then when it comes to time spent apart from our spouse, we only need to look at how Christ treated the church. In His time on earth, He only separated himself from His disciples to invest time with the Father through prayer and fasting. If our current schedules do not allow us to have quality time with our spouse and family each week, we can pray for God to show us how to unify our schedules, and He will make a way. Let us determine today to prevent separation from our spouse as much as possible, and let it be the exception rather than the standard as the world has made it. We determine our habits today, and our habits will determine our future!

SHARING AFFECTION

Another area of importance within marriage is found in I Corinthians 7:4, which says, *"The wife does not have authority over her own body, but the husband does. And like-*

wise the husband does not have authority over his own body, but the wife does." We see that when we entered into the marriage covenant with our spouse, our body then became our spouse's and we entrusted this very personal aspect of our lives to our spouse. With this trust and authority, a husband trusts his wife to be *willing* to be the sole provider of meeting his sexual needs. As a loving husband he would never demand this of her, and as a believer who loves and obeys God, he would not go outside the marriage, but would rather look to God for grace and strength if this need were going unmet. Likewise, in making the marriage covenant, the wife trusts her husband to be the provider of the *"affection due her"* as stated in 1 Corinthians 7:3, as well as to be the sole provider of her sexual needs.

If we look into the history of these Scriptures, we find that Paul wrote them to the Corinthians. Paul had found out some of the married believers in Corinth had adopted a radical position, believing that married couples should become celibate to completely focus their attention on serving God.[3] Paul wrote the Scriptures of 1 Corinthians 7:3-5 to address and correct these dangerous viewpoints which are in error to the Word of God and very deceptive lies Satan tried to use to bring temptation and destruction to the marriage relationship. Paul makes it very clear in 1 Corinthians 7:3-5 that within the marriage relationship, we should have a healthy, consistent, loving physical relationship.

AMY: MORE ON AFFECTION

As with sexual intimacy, it is difficult to share affection with our spouse when separated by distance. 1 Corinthians 7:3 states *"Let the husband render to his wife the affection due her, and likewise also the wife to her husband."* I greatly enjoyed when Shaun found this Scripture in the early years of our marriage and got very excited about it. He studied and meditated on it. He asked me what affection was to me. When ministering to another man on the topic of marriage, Shaun will often mention this Scripture. He makes sure men understand the importance of affection to a female, and he encourages them to ask their own wife for her personal definition.

To many women, affection means showing tenderness and love in tangible ways such as hugs, hand-holding, kisses, intimate conversation, holding each other, back rubs, and foot rubs, with no strings attached. In other words, affection is just to show her you love her, not intending to get a sexual response from her every time these things are given. To most women, affection is part of a daily environment they want to live in. Marriage and relationship expert Dr. Gary Smalley says people need eight to ten meaningful touches a day in order to maintain a healthy relationship.[4]

We once heard a story about a man and woman who went to a counselor. The wife was unhappy in the marriage and said her husband was not affectionate and never made time for her. The husband told the doctor that he did not see the point of affection. Holding hands, snuggling, it all had no purpose to him unless it was suppose to lead to "something else." The counselor thought for a moment and said, "Tell me, how would you feel if your wife told you that from now on she only wanted to have sexual intimacy when you were trying to have a baby, but once you are done having a baby, forget it. She just did not see any purpose for it anymore." Suddenly, the light bulb went on in the husband's head. With a surprised look he said, "Oh, I get it! It's purpose enough that she enjoys it." The wise counselor brought about a quick change of heart by relating the wife's need to something the husband could identify with.

SHAUN AND AMY:
LIVING TO PLEASE THE LORD

Throughout generations, there has at times been misunderstanding in the church as to how a married couple is to live according to 1 Corinthians 7:29,

But this I say, brethren, the time is short, so that from now on even those who have wives should be as though they had none.

Did Paul mean a husband should just forget he has a wife and children and leave home to do the work God has called him to do, only returning home long enough to get his wife pregnant, give her a little money, and then leave again? If this Scripture is carefully studied, it doesn't appear this is what Paul is saying here. Even if God calls a husband or wife to travel for ministry, they still have the responsibility of tending to their family and ensuring their home life stays in order. In fact, according to 1 Timothy 3:4-5, someone should not have a position as an overseer in the church unless he keeps his home life and family well maintained. Therefore, if someone is truly appointed by God to travel and it is not feasible for their spouse to go along, perhaps because of children in school, God's will is for quality relationships to still be maintained within the family. This is best achieved through consistently showing our spouse and children that we honor and value them deeply in whatever ways make them feel valued and loved, which may be completely different from what makes us feel valued and loved.

So what is Paul really saying through this admonition? Let us look at this Scripture in light of the other Scripture Paul has also written to determine his true intent. In 1 Corinthians 7:32, Paul goes on to say,

But I want you to be without care. He who is unmarried cares for the things of the Lord—how he may please the Lord. But he who is married cares about the things of the world—how he may please is wife.

He ends this topic by stating his purpose in saying all of this is *"...that you may serve the Lord without distraction"* (1 Corinthians 7:35).

The true intent of this portion of Scripture is found through understanding the word *"care."* The original word translated care in the first sentence, *"But I want you to be without care,"* meant to be without carefulness, in other words, "not anxious" and to be "secure" (Strong's #275). The other words translated "care" from the original Greek text meant either "to be anxious about' or "to take thought" (Strong's #3309). Therefore, is it wrong to please your wife or husband? No. If it were wrong, Paul would not have invested time earlier in the chapter admonishing husbands to meet their wife's needs for affection and also instructing that a husband and wife should be having regular sexual relations so that neither of them is tempted to go outside the marriage. Rather, Paul is teaching that it is wrong to have anxiety about pleasing our spouse.

Anxiety and worry about the marriage would cause a person to become distracted from the things of God. Instead, Paul is saying we as married people should take thought for how we can please God and fulfill his great commission to *"Go into all the world and preach the gospel to every creature"* (Mark 16:15).

People who live worldly lives frequently have much care and anxiety over their marriage. They are often insecure in their relationship because they can only place their trust in a person, and, as current divorce statistics show, people can let us down. As believers, on the other hand, we are to look to God rather than a person for our security. If the other person would stop following or obeying Christ for some reason, we can still be secure, knowing Christ will always see us through, no matter what. We as Christians do not need to have anxiety about our marriage like people in the world may, because our confidence is in Christ. We should exercise the genuine and giving love of God toward our spouse without anxiety. Then we will truly be able to focus on understanding God's plans and work together as a couple to further the Gospel of Christ.

OTHER FORMS OF SEPARATION

Let us also look at some other frequently unnoticed forms of marital separation. Todd works 40 to 50 hours per week providing for his family. He loves his family, but on evenings and weekends, he really feels a need for recreation to unwind from the pressures of his job. He likes playing baseball on a couple of leagues, and on weekends he enjoys fishing and hunting with the guys. Then there is Sherry. She puts in 60 to 70 hours a week at her new business to get it off the ground. She comes home and is exhausted. She usually heads straight to bed. She has not had time for her husband in quite a while and doesn't even know what is going on in the life of her children or who they are with, but she tells herself it will not always be this way.

Without realizing it, both of these people are neglecting their family, often unaware that it will most likely have repercussions on their marriage and cause rebellion and heartache in their children. Ideally, it would be great if both spouses would work together to fix these situations. A husband and wife can work to build a team mindset of being each other's best friend and looking for ways to make things great for everyone involved. This is not likely to happen without quality time together, maintaining some similar interests and having some activities together. This may mean the wife learning how to fish and the husband occasionally going shopping with a smile on his face.

Remember your dating days? You just wanted to be together for the sake of being with each other. It did not matter what you were doing. We can stir up those old emotions if they aren't there anymore. Invest time thinking about why you fell in love with your spouse and what your favorite qualities are about them. Look at old pictures, reflect on great memories, and start dreaming of new opportunities you can enjoy together in the future.

In the case of a new business or heavy work load, set a goal for when to start cutting back to more reasonable hours and make plans for how you can do more delegating. If possible, make your spouse and children a part of the new business venture. Children are often more helpful than one realizes if trained, given opportunity, and praised for their assistance. It is important to help our spouse and family feel a part of what we are doing.

If your spouse and family cannot physically be a part of the vision, be sure to update them with details on the progress of it and let them know your gratefulness for their support and that you couldn't build this dream without them. It is much more rewarding to get to the top and still have your family with you than to be at the top and have no one with whom to enjoy it.

KEEPING UNITY WITH OUR SPOUSE

If we must be apart from our family for a time, whether overnight or through a work schedule with long hours for several months, there are numerous kindnesses we can show to minimize the negative impact of separation. One pastor we know of, married over 50 years, is an excellent demonstration of our first suggestion. We were amazed and impressed to hear him say that when he must travel to preach without his wife, he typically calls her three times a day for prayer together and conversation. Praying together is an excellent way to keep the spiritual bond close, especially when separated by the miles.

Second, remember your spouse is your lover. Appreciation, admiration, and compliments should not go out the window with marriage and are especially important when separated for a time. This can be done through phone calls, emails, or notes sent in luggage or left at home in places they will find. Shaun will occasionally leave little sticky notes with loving messages around the house for me even when he is just at work, and I love this.

Third, we can daily jot down a few things we are thankful for or love about our spouse and read these to them on the phone or give the list to them upon returning from a trip. The more we focus on and remind ourselves of the good qualities our spouse has, the more we will value them and keep a right heart toward them while apart.

This is vital because the tendency of the flesh is to want to focus on negative things rather than positive things. If we intentionally choose to concentrate on the positive about our spouse, as well as in life, it will eventually become a habit and seem natural to focus on good things. When we keep a thankful heart toward our spouse it will also cause them to be more excited to return home because they are reminded that they have a loving family to come home to!

It is also a great idea to plan something special for when our spouse returns from a trip. Having something to look forward to will make the time apart less difficult on the family and build romance in the marriage relationship. It is always good to give our spouse a warm welcome home, causing them to see how much they are valued and appreciated.

We recently heard a story from an evangelist's daughter who said that when her dad traveled each week, her mom would spend the whole week talking and planning with her about the party they would have that weekend when her dad got home. She said that she never resented his being gone each week because she had so much fun planning a party for him every weekend when he returned.

Lastly, it is wise to never have anyone of the opposite sex over while your spouse is gone. What seems to begin harmlessly has many times turned into the fall of a marriage. We have heard stories of men asking their best friend to lend a helping hand to their wife while they were away on military duty so that no men pursued her. Sadly, some of these same men have returned home six months later to find divorce papers and their wife engaged to their best friend. If they do not guard their heart, many women have a tendency to develop feelings for a man who takes care of them financially or physically or who makes time to listen or compliment them. This is why phone and email conversations are important when apart. It meets a wife's need for verbal affection and attention.

KEEPING OUR KIDS' HEARTS CLOSE

As with our spouse, it is essential to maintain a loving relationship with our children at all times, including when time is spent apart. One of the biggest keys to maintaining a relationship is to know what makes the other person feel loved. It may be time together, gifts, affection, words of appreciation, or something else. A basic key to remember with our spouse or children is that men thrive on respect and women thrive on love (see Ephesians 5:33).

We have a close friend who is one of the best parents we have ever met. She has three beautiful daughters who are currently between ages 15 and 23. They all love the Lord and are some of the most loving, considerate, thoughtful, honest, selfless, and sincere young ladies we have ever met. In addition to all that, they are extremely intelligent, motivated, talented, and beautiful. One of the most outstanding characteristics the three daughters have is their deep loyalty and respect for their mother. This respect is not just there by happenstance. It has been cultivated consistently over many years by a very wise and loving mother. Let us share a few of her secrets to great parenting with you.

People often feel valued through traditions that make them feel important. This mom has many of those traditions. Many years ago, the mom purchased a red plate and started having a monthly dinner called "The Red Plate Dinner." Each month, a different member of the family gets the red plate. Whoever gets the red plate receives special honor and appreciation at the meal that evening. During or after the meal, they go around the table and everyone tells things they love, appreciate, and respect about that member of the family! Her girls love and look forward to this night every month. It serves a twofold purpose: in addition to building them up if it is their night, it also teaches the other family members to verbally place value on and esteem others. The honor and value we place on someone consistently with our words and actions will become an equal measure to the commitment they have in their hearts toward us!

When her girls were young this mom also started a tradition of having a tea party together every Friday when they would get home from school. This is just a simple way that their mom consistently shows them she values her time with them. It gives the girls opportunity to talk, which most women and girls like to do.

There are numerous ways that parents, including those who travel and sometimes work long hours, can show honor to their children. A once-a-month fishing or camping outing or making time to play catch with a ball once or twice a week may be just what makes kids feel loved by dad or mom. Whatever you choose, be sure it makes your child feel valued, and make sure you do it consistently. Children need consistent and tangible displays of honor and love. Throughout the week, keep the focus on what you plan to do together, and then make sure you always follow through with it.

If you or your spouse travel often, make every effort you can to travel together and even bring your children whenever possible. Make sure those you love know how much you love them. It is essential to a good relationship to make sure each person in our family knows we honor and value them. Ask them what makes them feel honored and valued. Study them to see what they do to show others love and you will probably have found what makes them feel loved.

God's best is for us to have strong families and maintain closeness with them. When we consistently do and say things to show our family members that they are in our heart, they will feel honored and valued and be committed to us in their heart.

Keeping The Family Together

1. Quality time together makes the heart grow fonder.
2. Pray diligently for your spouse to be protected from temptations when you have to be apart overnight.
3. Make scheduled time for each other and children throughout the week to keep your relationships strong.
4. Ask your spouse and children what makes them feel valued and be sure to meet this need on a weekly basis.

Chapter 10

The Friendship Reflection

**The righteous should choose his friends carefully,
for the way of the wicked leads them astray
(Proverbs 12:26).**

The saying, "Show me the ten people you hang around the most and I will show you where you will be in ten years," is extremely accurate. The quality of your marriage and family will eventually become a reflection of the people you surround yourself with. Do you want to be a success in your walk with God, the best spouse and parent you can be, and fulfill the call of God on your life?

A large portion of achieving these valuable life treasures requires cultivating Christ-like friendships and being receptive to mutual accountability through those friendships. It also includes accepting and receiving insight and correction from authority figures and mentors that God places in our life. When we are receptive to our mentor's instruction and have Christ-like friends, we will find ourselves increasingly walking in the promises of God. In doing this, we will greatly improve our relationships in the home and achieve greater levels of leadership in our place of work or ministry.

Friendships are just what the word describes. A friend is like a ship. They either help carry us up stream or down stream. Their words and actions have a large impact on us, negative or positive. Do our friends talk about and focus on the good in their spouse? We will be more likely to think and talk about our spouse in a positive way. Do they find fault in their spouse? If we continue to spend time with them, we will eventually begin to find fault in our spouse. Words spoken by those we are close to eventually influence us, producing either good or bad fruit in our lives. It is wise to invest time with those who realize they will eat the fruit of their lips; therefore, they speak with wisdom and are guarded in what they say.

We as believers are to be like eagles. Isaiah 40:31 states,

But those who wait on the Lord shall renew their strength; they shall mount up with wings as eagles, they shall run and not be weary, they shall walk and not faint.

God wants us to soar above life's circumstances. Our close friendships (or lack of Christ-like friendships) will greatly influence how high we soar.

Have you ever studied the great difference between the life of Samson and the life of David? Both were called by God to have a leadership position among their people and were considered men of great faith. Samson, however, accomplished very little of lasting worth compared to David. Samson did not undertake the task of organizing and leading the Israelites to deliver them from the Philistines. Instead he performed a few exploits that exalted himself against the Philistines, rather than exalting his nation.

In contrast, David organized troops, planned and strategized, sought the Lord's direction, was king for many years, left a lasting impact for generations to come, and made a large majority of good decisions in his lifetime. What do you think made the difference? Certainly, many things could be factored in to this difference in success, but we would like to focus on one characteristic that we believe played a large role.

THE LIFE OF SAMSON

In everything recorded about Samson, there is nothing spoken of his having any friends. It even states that when Samson gave his marriage feast, the Philistines brought 30 male companions to celebrate with him, which leaves us to wonder, why did Samson not have any friends of his own? Throughout the entire account of Samson, in addition to nothing being spoken of his having any personal friends, there is also nothing spoken of his having accountability to anyone, such as advisors or mentors.

As we study the passages of Judges 14 -16, we find Samson, who had a great call of God on his life, pursuing his own pleasures and not allowing anyone to become close enough to speak into his life. Samson's choices caused a very tragic end to his life. Proverbs 18:1 seems to characterize the life of Samson: *"A man who isolates himself seeks his own desire; he rages against all wise judgment."* A common thread we find throughout the entire Bible is that God's plan for order always includes accountability through other people, which Samson regularly ignored.

THE LIFE OF DAVID

On the opposite side, we find David. Also called by God at a young age to lead his people, David made his best efforts to surround himself with wise counsel and faithful friends. In 1 Samuel 23:16-17, we find one of the greatest and most profound accounts of friendship a person could experience.

Then Jonathan, Saul's son, arose and went to David in the woods and strengthened his hand in God. And he said to him, "Do not fear, for the hand

of Saul my father shall not find you. You shall be king over Israel, and I shall be next to you. Even my father Saul knows that."

Jonathan was such a true friend that he chose not to be jealous when God had selected David to rule the kingdom, rather than allowing Saul's lineage to continue on the throne. Naturally, Jonathan himself would have been heir to the throne, yet he cheerfully acknowledged in this passage of Scripture that David was suppose to have the position. Not only that, but it also states that Jonathan strengthened David's hand in God, meaning he encouraged and built up his friend David during this time of adversity in his life.

In 2 Samuel 12 we find another trusted friend, Nathan the prophet, going to King David to rebuke him for having an affair with Bathsheba and then having her husband killed. Nathan must have been in close standing with the king to have been allowed into his presence freely. David accepted his wise friend's correction and had genuine, lasting repentance. Later, in 2 Samuel 17, we find another close friend, Hushai, risking his own life to protect and help David to safety. There are numerous other men that David had acquired as close friends and counselors. It would certainly be fair to say that through these friends, the Lord frequently worked to protect David as well as get him back on the right path when he had gone astray into sin.

Truly, one of David's most outstanding characteristics was that he allowed people to get close to him who were wise, discerning, and loved him deeply. He accepted correction as well as help from those people when he needed it. He wanted to please God, so he would change what he needed to change and then press on. We can all learn from David's example. As David's son Solomon stated in Proverbs 11:14, *"Where there is no counsel, the people fall; but in the multitude of counselors there is safety."*

CHRIST-LIKE FRIENDS

Let us focus our attention to how the Word of God describes a true or Christ-like friend. First, a Christ-like friend will above all else be a friend of Christ. Jesus was the ultimate example of friendship when He laid down His life for us in order to bring us back to right standing with God. Jesus taught in John 15:12-15,

This is My commandment, that you love one another as I have loved you. Greater love has no one than this, than to lay down one's life for his friends. You are my friends if you do whatever I command you. No longer do I call you servants, for a servant does not know what his master is doing; but I have called you friends, for all things

that I heard from My Father I have made known to you.

We recognize from this that the first way to discern if someone is a Christ-like friend is to observe the person's love walk. If someone has a close relationship with the Lord, they will be growing more and more in His commandment to love. There will be fruit that demonstrates the love of God in their life. Even when someone makes a mistake, it is apparent how mature their love walk is by how quickly they repent and apologize for a wrong done to another and move forward in the Word to ensure they do the right thing next time.

We once heard a speaker say that years ago she decided to take a very close look at herself. She was moving up in her profession and observing those she wanted to emulate in the company, as well as those she would like to develop friendships with one day. She asked herself, "What kind of person am I? What kind of friend am I?"

When she thought about the answer to these questions, she remembered having once heard that you can know what is in your heart by what spills out when you get bumped. In other words, when we are put under pressure or someone does not treat us right, how do we react? If we are at a restaurant and the waiter messes up our order, do we get irritated or do we respond with patience and kindness, using it as an opportunity to show mercy and grace?

As she reflected, she realized that often times what was spilling out of her wasn't very nice. She chose to change herself with diligent study in the Word and prayer. Today she is a wonderful example of a Christian, at the top in her profession, a spiritual and professional mentor to many, and she has the kind of friends she once longed for. She realized that to be a great leader, as well as to have quality friends who walk in the love of God, she first had to become a person who walked in the love of God herself.

STICKING CLOSER THAN A BROTHER

A Christ-like friend is one *"...who sticks closer than a brother"* (Proverbs 18:24). True friends will be there to help each other when tough times come. It may be a word of encouragement based on Scripture, a helping hand, or some other means of support. This kind of person is also the type that will correct his friend if he sees him getting off course from the Word and plan of God. In other words, he will confront with love. Sometimes friends will be the first to notice traps the enemy has set. A true friend will be more concerned about our staying on track with God than they are about offending us. They will diligently pray for their friend and bring correction as the Lord leads.

We recently had someone share her personal testimony with us of a time when she had gone off track from the plan of God in a big way and had problems in her marriage. She credited one of her friends for being an instrument of God to correct her when she didn't want to follow God. She said her friend was loving yet firm about what was right. Her friend gave her correction through the Word combined with genuine love, and through this, she chose to follow God's plan for her life rather than the enemy's agenda.

IRON SHARPENING IRON

A true friend is an "iron-sharpening-iron" friend. Proverbs 27:17 states, *"As iron sharpens iron, so a man sharpens the countenance of his friend."* Iron is known for being a strong building material. Therefore, two friends who are building themselves strong in the Word of God will come together to encourage and strengthen one another in the Lord. They will continually be building on, drawing out, and sharpening each other in a way that causes each one to produce greater spiritual fruit, becoming more useful for God's kingdom.

This is one of the reasons Hebrews 10:25 says we as believers should be *"...not forsaking the assembling of ourselves together, as is the manner of some, but exhorting one another, and so much the more as you see the Day approaching."* God knows that the more we go to a great Bible-teaching church, we will encourage others, and others will encourage us in the promises of God. When we leave the presence of Godly people, we should have our countenance lifted, and they should have theirs lifted from having been with us. We should leave believing and acting upon the Scripture that states, *"I can do all things through Christ who strengthens me"* (Philippians 4:13).

A classic example of two iron-sharpening-iron friends is Joshua and Caleb. In Numbers 13 and 14 we find the story of the twelve tribal leaders going to spy out the land God told them they were to possess. Ten of the men brought back an evil report. On the other hand, in verses 6 and 7, we see Joshua and Caleb together speaking to all of Israel. Joshua and Caleb did their best to convince the people that they were well able to do what God said they could do and able to have what God said they could have. It appears that Joshua and Caleb invested time together as friends. Otherwise, they would not be mourning together, because they knew the Israelites' unbelief was a sin before God.

The ten leaders with an evil report all died in the wilderness along with those who believed their evil report. In other words, these ten men were not successful in their leadership roles. As leaders they steered their ship downstream instead of upstream, which resulted in the people failing in God's plan for their life.

Joshua and Caleb, however, refused to participate in negative talk or unbelief. They were true leaders. Since Joshua and Caleb's first group of followers chose not to receive God's report, God let that whole generation die and gave the two men the next generation to lead into the Promised Land, people who were strong, courageous and determined to possess the promises of God! Joshua and Caleb never gave up, and they eventually gained their victory.

MENTORING FRIENDS

Another type of friend is the one who mentors another in the things of God. As one body in Christ, we are to help each other function and improve, just as the human body parts help each other function. In Titus 2:4, Paul discusses with his young assistant and ministry partner the importance of the older women in the church teaching, mentoring, and admonishing the younger women to do good, love their husbands, and love their children. A good mentor is a precious treasure in the life of a believer.

It is important to remember that we can all learn from someone, no matter how old we are in the Lord. To think we have arrived or that we are at a place so far ahead spiritually that we cannot learn from others anymore is prideful. It is like the head saying to the feet, "I have no need of you" (see 1 Corinthians 12:21). God places others in our path to be a gift to us and places us in the path of others to be a gift to them.

We once heard a very wise and experienced pastor say the reason so many young pastors quickly fizzle out in ministry is that they rush into their own ministry rather than taking time to be mentored by an experienced pastor. There is a wealth of knowledge to be gained from a victorious, mature Christian who has learned to consistently walk in the love of God. Mentors impart truth to others through teaching and being an example, bringing the one being mentored to a higher place in the Lord. Mentors also exhort, encourage, and lovingly correct when needed.

If someone is mentoring you, also remember that relationships are intended to go both ways. Therefore, always be looking for ways to be a gift to your mentor. This may be through prayer, physical assistance with the ministry (as Titus and Timothy assisted Paul), or through numerous other ways the Lord can reveal to you by His Spirit.

PEOPLE TO BE WARY OF

Have you ever met someone who has tremendous potential, but never accomplishes much in his or her life? They live in mediocrity and continue to settle for the "short end of the stick." If we take a close look into their lives, the majority of the time we will find unhealthy relationships. Negative people will try to keep others from fulfilling their dreams, unlike a good friend who will build up and encourage you in the plan and call of God. Be wary of those who find fault and condemn others. Those who allow negative and critical friends into their lives eventually become negative and critical themselves. As Proverbs 13:20 states, *"He who walks with wise men will be wise, but the companion of fools will be destroyed."*

We would like to add here that if you are married to a negative person, don't lose hope! It is important to fight the fight of faith through prayer, speaking Scripture over your spouse and applying faith to the situation. If they are a believer, pray and ask God to help them increase in yielding to the Holy Spirit's joy, as well as to other fruits of the Spirit. People who are led by the Spirit walk in the fruits of the Spirit.

Being married to a negative person is a great opportunity to practice being a doer of the Word. As you speak the Word over your spouse, practice rejoicing when you go through challenges in life (see 1 Thessalonians 5:16-18). Also remember, if rejoicing were an easy thing to do at these times, God would not have had to instruct us to do it. If your spouse is negative, remember to be like David. When his men were all very upset with him, it says that David *"... strengthened himself in the Lord his God"* (1 Samuel 30:6).

When we consistently place our hope and trust in God through speaking His Word over our spouse, rather than accepting what we hear and see in our spouse, we will be able to remain in peace and allow God to work on our behalf. Proverbs 16:20 says, *"... Whoever trusts in the Lord, happy is he."* When our trust is in God, we can refuse to entertain discouragement, no matter how hard it knocks on our door. Instead, we choose to keep our eyes and words on His promises. Then God is able to send His help.

WORLDLY FRIENDS

When we choose to be close friends with those who want one foot in the church and one foot in the world, we place ourselves in danger of falling into the same patterns. As 1 John 2:15 states, *"Do not love the world or the things in the world. If anyone loves the world, the love of the Father is not in him."* Paul told the Corinthians, *"Do you not know that a little leaven leavens the whole lump? Therefore purge out the old leaven, that you may be a new lump, since you truly are unleavened"* (1 Corinthians 5:6-7). He was saying here that we should choose to surround ourselves with those who want to grow in their walk with God, rather than those who choose to stay in their old sins.

What do we do if we currently have worldly friends? Of course the best thing is to witness to them and hopefully they ask Jesus into their heart and choose to live for Him. However, if this does not happen, we have personally found, and also seen in others that it is usually necessary to leave close friendship with that person behind us. We have witnessed new believers who were so determined to lead their old friends to the Lord, but instead they ended up going back to their old ways because they kept hanging around the old friends when they were sinning.

In the body of Christ there is a lot of talk about what is called "friendship evangelism." The whole concept behind this is great. It is only when people create their own definition of friendship evangelism, choosing to justify their fleshly desire not to separate themselves from things of the world that this becomes a problem.

Jesus was a wonderful example to us of how true "friendship evangelism" works through loving others and ministering to them. However, when Jesus pursued winning the lost, he did so during his daily life encounters, such as conversation about God over a shared meal. He never went down to the local gambling place and sat with them while they played poker and listened to them tell perverse jokes. He didn't try to get to know them on their turf, while they were in the middle of practicing their sin, and then attempt to get them saved. This doesn't work because going somewhere with an unbeliever to watch them sin is telling them we don't have enough personal conviction to stay away from the world ourselves.

TIME STEALERS

Other friends to be on guard of are those who steal time from our spouse and family. The enemy will try to busy us in any way he can. If we are not watchful, it is very easy to fall into this trap in the fast-paced society we live. If we keep a full schedule of activities, hobbies, sports, or even talking on the telephone with our friends on evenings and weekends, we end up leaving little time for our loved ones.

Our time investments reflect our true priorities in life. When we look at our schedule over the last month, do our time commitments demonstrate that our spouse and family come before activities, work, friends, and extended family, or is the opposite true? If friends, hobbies, sports, TV, or computer have time priority, what are our actions telling our spouse and children about how much value we place on them? Valuing a person is part of honoring them. God told us in His Word to show honor to our loved ones because He knew honor is vital to maintaining a healthy, mutually fulfilling relationship.

We have personally found it necessary to schedule time together as a couple and a family each week, otherwise the week often slips by. Years ago I had the privilege in one of my very first ministry classes to study under a professor who had retired from 50 years of highly successful ministry. I'll never forget what he shared with us. He said to remember when we become pastors, that first and foremost we are ministers to God; second only to God we are ministers to our family; and thirdly we are ministers to the congregation God gives us (which includes friends). He then said that every week he made plans with his family and when someone called to try to get him to schedule a meeting or do something else during that time slot he would say, "I apologize, my appointment book is already full at that time." His family date was always priority.

TRAPS TO AVOID

As a couple, be cautious of doing everything with other couples and not having any alone time or private dates. Friends are wonderful, but it is important for us to remember we are not married to them. They should not be with us all of the time. Some personalities like to surround themselves with other people continually. However, in order to cultivate and maintain a quality, close relationship with our spouse, it requires private date and talk time each week.

Also, remember friends and family are not a forum for us to tell on our spouse whenever they make a mistake or disagree with us. We would be wise to treat our spouse with the same courtesy we would like to receive ourselves. When an issue arises, wisdom knows that making our spouse feel secure in the relationship is of utmost importance. Tale bearing brings division with our spouse and builds feelings of insecurity rather than unity, which is essential to a great marriage.

If we consistently have unresolved marital issues, we can ask our spouse if they will go with us to a pastor or mentor-type couple who is successful in their marriage to discuss the issues and get advice. If they are not yet willing to seek help, be patient. When we go to God with a humble heart and pray that He will help us to walk in His love toward our spouse, He is faithful to teach us the things we need to know and do.

Then when our spouse notices a new effort in our life, they may be more willing to get help in the relationship.

GOD HAS GOOD PLANS FOR YOU

Remember God has a good plan for you, to give you a hope and a future (see Jeremiah 29:11). Jesus desires to be your best friend! All we need to do is give Him time each day with His Word, prayer, and fellowship, listening to what His Holy Spirit has to say to our heart. He will reveal His plan for you and your family. He has placed a very important call on your life that only you can fulfill in the earth. No one else can do exactly what He has called you to do because He made you an original. As the Psalmist so perfectly states,

I will praise You, for I am fearfully and wonderfully made; marvelous are Your works, and that my soul knows very well (Psalm 139:14).

As you choose to walk in God's good plans for you, which include being a Christ-like friend to others and accepting Christ-like friends into your life, God will have a special avenue through those friends to encourage and strengthen you. He will be able to work through you to do the same for others.

As you select your friends, always remember Proverbs 12:26, *"The righteous should choose his friends carefully, for the way of the wicked leads them astray."* Make a conscious choice today to submit to God's plan for your friendships. Just as Joshua and Caleb stuck together in the midst of the people and inherited the promises of God for their families, we believe that each day, as you choose to surround yourself with Christ-like friends and be a Christ-like friend, you will also find yourself living in the Promised Land God has for you.

<u>Choosing The Right Friends</u>
1. Don't let just anyone be close to you.
2. Choose your friends carefully.
3. Be a Christ-like friend.
4. Look for iron-sharpening-iron friends.
5. Accept mentoring friendships as the Lord leads.

Chapter 11

How to Overcome
Sexual Temptations

**For the law of the Spirit of life in Christ Jesus
has made me free from the law of sin and death
(Romans 8:2).**

We once heard a story about a pastor who lived in England many years ago. He was asked to visit an old woman from his congregation who was nearing the end of her life. During his visit with her at her tiny, rundown shack in an extremely poor part of town, he noticed one small, framed paper hanging on her wall. He went to look at it and asked her what it was. She told him that she had been a personal servant to one of the women of nobility in England for many years. When the woman she worked for was on her deathbed, one of the last things she did was giving her that paper. The lady went on to say that she had always treasured the paper, so she had found a frame for it and hung it on her wall.

The pastor asked the lady if he could borrow it for a few days and have it looked at by someone. When he took it to authorities, they asked him where he had found this and said they had been looking for it for many years. It turned out that the woman from his church could not read, so she never knew that the paper the woman had given her was a certified document entitling her to an inheritance. The woman had provided her with a home and money that would have taken care of her the rest of her life. Since this old woman did not know that she owned all of this, the house and money just sat there all of those years while she lived in a tiny old shack with barely enough food to eat.

You may be asking yourself, "What could this story possibly have to do with a believer overcoming sexual addictions and immorality?" Quite a bit actually, because this story is a perfect example of what happens when a believer doesn't know what belongs to them in their inheritance through Jesus Christ. They fail to possess their God-given rights of the law of the Spirit of life and live in the blessing of it.

Just as this old woman did not know she had an inheritance that entitled her to live an abundant life, many believers do not realize that Jesus has already provided us with an inheritance that entitles us to live free from bondage to sin. We do not have to earn this freedom but only freely and boldly accept what Jesus did for us. The same power that raised Him from the dead lives in us; therefore, we can daily live victorious over the power of sin and death. Jesus died on the cross to break the power of the law of sin and death that Satan held over mankind. He stripped Satan of all the power Adam and Eve had given to him through their disobedience in the Garden of Eden, and He freely gave that dominion back to us as believers! In doing so, He brought the law of the Spirit of life into operation, which overrides the law of sin and death.

WHY DO TEMPTATIONS COME?

Satan does not send temptations to someone just to try to destroy their marriage. If this were the case, then only married people would be tempted. Satan tries to send temptations to everyone, married or not, because his main goal is "... *to steal, kill, and destroy,*" as John 10:10 states. He tries to keep a person from discovering their rights in Jesus and tries to steal the Word of God out of a believer's heart because he knows that the truth will set people free. Anyone with the Word of God in their heart gains knowledge and access to their ability to live free from strongholds themselves. They are then able to teach others so that they can live free and be delivered from Satan's rule.

Jesus is to be our ultimate example because the Bible says He was in all ways tempted as we are, yet without sin. That is good news! This means it is possible for us to live a victorious life, free from sin. When we choose to keep Christ first place in our life, we know that even if temptation knocks on the door, we can say no and refuse to open the door. Someone else's failures or even our own failures should in no way influence our belief in the Word and the power the Word brings to live a victorious life. In other words, we must never let our own or others' experiences interpret what we believe from the Bible. Rather, we should seek to know the truth of the Bible and let it determine our experiences.

A highly successful evangelist once stated that in his early years of ministry he went up into the mountains to have time with God, and during this time he made a firm decision. He decided he was going to take God at His Word, no matter what. He was going to preach the Bible whether others believed it or not because he knew in his heart that the Word of God is true and has the power to transform lives.

When a person has made this decision in their heart, it brings them to a place of hearing someone's mistakes and saying, "They may have missed the mark, but I still know the Word is true and I choose to believe it. I am determined to walk in its promises whether anybody else does or not." Are God and His Word powerful enough to help His children be victorious over temptations? 1 Corinthians 10:13 gives us the answer.

No temptation has overtaken you except such as is common to man; but God is faithful, who will

not allow you to be tempted beyond what you are able, but with the temptation will also make the way of escape, that you may be able to bear it.

Therefore, we know when Satan brings temptation, God also comes on the scene and always has a way of escape. He provides the ability to resist the temptation. So why do so many people choose not to resist? We believe it is usually because they lack understanding of the Word and the means God has planned to resist and avoid sin. If a believer does not have God's Word in their heart on a consistent basis, they will not know what is available to them to resist, even though it was there all along. Let's take a close look at what means and direction God has provided in His Word for us to resist temptation so we can consistently walk free from the law of sin and death.

CONSISTENTLY STAYING OUT OF SEXUAL SIN

TRUTH #1...STRENGTHEN YOURSELF DAILY IN THE WORD

We know that whoever is born of God does not sin, but he who has been born of God keeps himself, and the wicked one does not touch him (1 John 5:18).

This Scripture sounds good, doesn't it? The wicked one not touching us, that is the place we all want to be! The word *touch* in the Greek text also means, "to attach oneself" (Strong's #680). Therefore, this is not implying that he or she who walks with God will not have attacks or trials in their life. It is saying that when those attacks or trials come, as long as we are keeping ourselves close to God (under the shadow of the Most High as Psalm 91 states), Satan will not be able to overpower us with his temptation and attach himself to us. What can a person do if those old sins have been attaching themselves? How is it that someone who is born of God keeps himself so the sins are resisted instead of attached? The answer is found in Romans 8:5-6.

For those who live according to the flesh set their minds on the things of the flesh, but those who live according to the Spirit, the things of the Spirit. For to be carnally minded is death, but to be spiritually minded is life and peace.

The key to keeping ourselves so the wicked one can't touch us is all in what we choose to set our mind on and thereby set our heart on. According to this, we see that someone who does evil or lives a fleshly life has first allowed the desire from the temptation to conceive in their mind and thereby allowed their mind to be set on fleshly or worldly thoughts. James 1:12-16 describes it this way,

Blessed is the man who endures temptation; for when he has been approved, he will receive the crown of life which the Lord has promised to those who love Him. Let no one say when he is tempted, 'I am tempted by God'; for God cannot be tempted by evil, nor does He Himself tempt anyone. But each one is tempted when he is drawn away by his own desires and enticed. Then, when desire has conceived, it gives birth to sin; and sin, when it is full-grown, brings forth death. Do not be deceived, my beloved brethren.

From this passage of Scripture, we know sexual immorality is not something that suddenly jumps into someone's mind one day and they go and act it out immediately. A thought or desire first comes to the mind. Then, rather than the thought being rejected as not good and cast down, it is conceived through the person beginning to entertain it in their thought life. Often these thoughts initially come through seeing a movie, television show, reading a book, or through a co-worker.

Someone may have an affair in a movie and they make it look so fun and harmless, like it is the answer to a boring life. A book may tell of a certain marital problem someone had and say the couple ended up getting divorced because of it. Maybe a well-meaning friend of someone with a bad marriage says "You deserve to be happy," implying divorce is the answer to a happy life. These are all thoughts that must be cast down in the name of Jesus and the source of them avoided; otherwise, they will conceive in the mind and eventually give birth to sin.

Someone who is born of God is to live by the Spirit, which means that we keep our mind set on things of the Spirit. The first thing we must do to live by the Spirit is to renew our mind in His Word daily. People we know who have gotten into affairs or pornography are typically people who have let their daily Bible reading slip or never started it.

We strengthen our heart and build wisdom by seeking the Lord through His written Word, so that we are prepared before the temptations or potentially compromising situations arise. Wisdom knows that true and lasting joy comes only from God and cannot be attained through temporal things. God wants all of us to be happy, and He has a means of achieving this in our life. The difference is that the true happiness He brings will not cause pain to our family or us.

In addition to reading the Word and fellowshipping with God, there are other ways to keep our mind on things of the Spirit and keep sexual temptations out. One is to specifically meditate each day on a Scripture concerning this topic. Biblical meditation actually refers to speaking a verse. We personally like to repeat a Scripture a number of times, emphasizing different words in the verse. It is beneficial to even write the verse on a card and read it throughout the day.

The Bible says faith comes by hearing the Word of God, so the more we get into our heart what the Word says about sexual immorality, the easier it will be to avoid. Proverbs chapters 5-7 are excellent to meditate on every day. Also, listening to excellent preaching messages throughout the day or at night before going to bed is an effective way to keep our mind set on things of the Spirit and keep our hearts pure.

We once heard a pastor share a wonderful story about keeping the mind off worldly things and set on the Spirit. He said a well-respected businessman in his church a number of years ago came and talked to him about a pornography addiction he had been struggling with. The man was serious about getting rid of this sin, so the pastor recommended that in addition to keeping the man accountable and checking in with him every few months, the man should also remove all means that could possibly bring temptation.

This man came back to the pastor months later and told him that since his profession required travel, he asked his secretary to request the television be removed from his room before he checked in when she made his hotel reservations. One time he arrived and the TV was still in his room, so he unplugged it and carried it down to the front desk. He told the front desk attendant that he did not want the TV in his room during his stay there, but he would be happy to put it back when he left.

This man decided he would rather make himself a little uncomfortable or even embarrassed than get into sin and take the chance of possibly losing his wife and children. When we as believers are totally determined to set our mind on things that please God, rather than set our mind on things of the flesh, we are willing to take uncommon measures to protect our mind from sin. In the day we live, with sexual immorality abounding, we must be willing to take uncommon measures if we want to protect our family and ourselves.

One measure we have personally taken in our home, which may sound extreme to some, is that we don't watch any movie, TV show, or read any books of people doing anything that we would not feel good about doing ourselves. Why? Because what we continually see with our eyes will eventually affect our heart, and what gets in the heart will be acted out through word and action. If there is a person even flirting with someone other than their spouse and we were to watch it on TV, we know that we would eventually become desensitized to this and think it's not a big deal, so we choose not to watch it. If there are spouses or children being disrespectful to their family members, we choose not to watch it because we don't want to become desensitized to think a lack of respect is okay in our home. Whatever we allow our mind to be set on, fleshly or spiritual, will eventually dominate our heart as well as the outcome of our life.

TRUTH #2...SHUN THE APPEARANCE
OF EVIL

To be the best leader and spouse we can possibly be, and to protect our relationships, we must remove situations that have potential to bring about compromise in our workplace. People, particularly Christians, who get involved in sexual immorality are typically not people who set out with the intention to do so. They are often good-hearted people, but they were not regularly keeping their mind set on things of the Spirit. Unfortunately, they didn't realize that Satan was setting them up and they were about to take his bait.

A person often may not think anything of these things, such as lunches with co-workers, travel with co-workers, and private meetings behind closed doors with co-workers. However, as believers, we should always stop and ask ourselves, "Does this situation have the potential of appearing evil to anyone (especially my spouse) or leading to compromise?" If something could possibly have the appearance of evil, it provides opportunity for the devil to bring up false accusations, or worse yet, to bring in temptations.

We personally believe that ministries and ministers need to be even more cautious of this than others. It is wise for all, but especially those in ministry, to evaluate what could be done to eliminate potential for the appearance of evil in the work place. Could a window be added to an office wall?

Could a decision be made to send three people on business trips instead of two?

Many affairs that occur between co-workers happen for four reasons, we have seen: first, because people often have more quality time with their co-workers than they do their own family; second, because people at work usually see each other on their best and most polite behavior; third, because co-workers are often striving to reach a common goal and there is a bonding that often takes place (if not guarding the heart) when goals are achieved together; and fourth, co-workers are often placed in compromising situations for the sake of work. These compromising situations start out truly harmless, but then a feeling may creep up for a person that starts being entertained in the mind. If this occurs, then the meetings may become more intentional rather than work related. Before long, both parties may take the bait and step into the devil's trap.

If we will remember to not only shun evil but also even shun *the appearance* of evil, we will guard ourselves from these and many other potentially damaging situations. When someone is the head of a ministry, organization, or business, it is wise, as we mentioned earlier, to not only guard ourselves but also our employees against what could be a compromising situation. When leaders love what is good, they will do everything they can to protect themselves and those under their authority from even the appearance of evil.

TRUTH #3...HAVE AN ACCOUNTABILITY PARTNER

In situations we have worked with, as well as in documentation from Christian counselors we have studied, accountability to a strong Christian is an extremely effective tool in helping a person get rid of or stay out of immorality of any kind. The best accountability partners are those who are strong in the particular area themselves, confidential and trustworthy, and those who are also well respected by the one who is being accountable to them. Small groups can also be very effective if they have a strong leader.

A person should never be embarrassed about going to someone for help, no matter what the issue they are dealing with, as long as they know they can trust the person they are going to. Sometimes people get the idea that what they have gotten involved in or have been tempted to do is so bad they couldn't tell anyone, so either fear or pride tries to stop them from getting help. If you are ever in that situation, just ask yourself this question: Would I rather go to one trusted person for help and accountability with this sin I want out of my life, or would I rather have it published on tomorrow morning's newspaper headlines for the whole world to read? That should make the answer easy.

Satan is a deceiver. He tries to get people in fear, thinking that if their spouse finds out about the sin they are dealing with, they might leave them or it might hurt their spouse so much they couldn't handle it. The truth is, although a person's spouse may feel very hurt over these things and could even choose to leave them, there is no hope for a good marriage without honesty.

According to Scripture, family should stick with us through thick and thin, particularly if they are believers. Proverbs 17:17 even states, *"A friend loves at all times, and is born, as is a brother, for adversity"* (Amp). The New Living Translation says it this way, *"A friend is always loyal, and a brother is born to help in time of need."* The word adversity was translated from the Hebrew word "tsarah" which means "affliction, anguish, distress, tribulation, or trouble" (Strong's #6869). We can see then, that a brother (or sister) is born to help in times of affliction, distress, and tribulation. If God desires and expects a brother or sister to stand by us in times of trouble, how much more should our spouse with whom we have vowed to be one?

Some may say, "But Jesus said a person wasn't sinning if they divorced their spouse for committing fornication." (Fornication most often meant harlotry, but could also mean adultery.) Yes, this is true. But, notice that Jesus did not say a person *should* divorce their spouse for this. He simply said they weren't sinning if they did. Therefore, He was not saying that divorce is God's best answer for this kind of situation. God's best is always love and complete restoration of a family.

A person has to decide for him or herself whether they are willing to persevere in their marriage and look to God to help them forgive and love with His love when an affair has occurred (assuming the other spouse wants to work things out). Someone who is willing to do this loves their spouse like many people love their children, with God's kind of love. In some of the very best marriages we know of today, couples who are the most Christ-like, trustworthy, committed to each other, and totally-in-love people we know once had marriages that were on the brink of disaster because of an affair. We are so thankful those couples didn't give up.

We once heard a wonderful sermon on forgiving other Christians when they fall. The pastor talked about a movie from many years ago, *My Friend Flicka*. In the movie, the horse got hurt, but they loved that horse so much they nursed it back to health. The common thing in that day was to just shoot a horse if it was seriously injured. The pastor made the point that many Christians today have the common mind-set of that day. He said that if a Christian falls into sin we often just get angry with them and think, "How could they have done this?" Then he said, "What about Flicka? What about that deep love that is willing to see a person through to be restored?"

Ephesians 1:6 says that God, *"...made us accepted in the Beloved."* This means God chose to accept us into His kingdom just the way we were before we got saved because of what Jesus did on the cross for us. He didn't leave people in their sin. He makes people righteous through the precious blood of Jesus when they ask Him into their heart (see 2 Corinthians 5:21, Philippians 3:9). Then He shows them in His Word and with the help of His Holy Spirit how to live a life free from sin.

Since God is our example of love and He forgave us, it is wise for us to follow His lead and also do our part to help others out of sin. When we show love to others even when they make mistakes, it will build their trust for us. We can love people even when they have missed the mark and then help them get back on track with God. God describes having accountability partners this way:

Brethren, if a man is overtaken in any trespass, you who are spiritual restore such a one in a spirit of gentleness, considering yourself lest you also be tempted. Bear one another's burdens, and so fulfill the law of Christ (Galatians 6:1-2).

TRUTH #4... SHAUN:
THE SECRET PLACE PREVENTS HAVING
SECRETS TO HIDE

One thing I have desired of the Lord, that will I seek; that I may dwell in the house of the Lord all the days of my life, to behold the beauty of the Lord, and to inquire in His temple. For in the time

of trouble He shall hide me in His pavilion; in the secret place of His tabernacle He shall hide me; He shall set me high upon a rock (Psalm 27:4-5).

As the psalmist declared, when we seek the Lord every day of our life, having time in the secret place with Him, He is then able to set us on a high rock. The secret place means having uninterrupted time alone each day reading His Word, praying, and having quality time listening to His voice. Through this time, God is able to reveal secret things to us that will protect our family and us. He is able to strengthen us against attacks the devil has planned, causing us to be placed on a high rock, out of the devil's reach.

We remember one such time when the Lord revealed secret things to us for our protection. After my personal morning prayer time, I go pray with Amy. This certain morning I told her that I had a dream before I woke up. The Lord had shown me there was a man she worked with, and I told her what his name was in the dream, which had begun stopping at her desk to talk regularly and tell her sad stories about his personal life. The Lord had shown me that he was making most of the stories up just because he was interested in Amy and wanted an excuse to talk to her in an attempt to get her feeling sorry for him. (The devil attempts to play on a woman's emotions because most women are caregivers and relationship fixers). I advised her to make herself busy when he came around and not waste any time listening to him.

Amy confirmed that everything I said was true. There was a man she worked with by that name who had been talking to her about the exact things I said, word for word. She thanked me and said she would follow my advice. About two months later, Amy informed me that what the Lord had shown me was very accurate. She found out this man who had once been walking with the Lord, had now fallen from his relationship with God and was in sexual sin.

God is interested in the details of our lives. He wants to protect and keep us out of harm's way, but in order to do this, we must give Him opportunity to talk to us through investing time with Him. Our life is like a parade. God is up above and can see down on the whole parade from start to finish. As we go through life we usually can't see what is around the next corner because we are right in the middle of the parade. God, on the other hand, sees what is around every turn because He is watching from a high place.

He knows what He has planned for us, and He also knows what traps the devil has set in an attempt to throw us off course. When we give God quality time, He is then able to take us up to see our parade from His view for a moment in order to give us a glimpse of things we need to see. God can reveal any trap set by the enemy, and then we can just walk around it and stay on God's course!

Proverbs 7:1-5 reminds us of the importance of keeping God's Word in our heart at all times to protect ourselves and keep us on the right path.

My son, keep my words, and treasure my commands within you. Keep my commands and live, and my law as the apple of your eye. Bind them on your fingers; write them on the tablet of your heart. Say to wisdom, "You are my sister," and call understanding your nearest kin, that they may keep you from the immoral woman, from the seductress who flatters with her words.

This Scripture perfectly illustrates that when we invest time in the secret place, Satan won't be able to trap us into having any secrets to hide.

TRUTH #5…SHAUN AND AMY
KNOW THE COST OF SIN TO CHILDREN

2 Samuel 13 tells the story of King David's son Amnon violating his sister Tamar. Interestingly, this tragic story of incest told in chapter 13 begins in verse 1 with the two words, *"After this…"* and then goes on to tell what happened. "After this" is the writer making sure the reader knows there was a precedent or something that led up to this. What led up to this incident happening in King David's home? If we read the prior two chapters, we discover the story of David committing adultery with Bathsheba. Therefore, the writer wants to make sure we, the reader, understand that these two incidents are closely connected to one another.

Why are they closely connected? When David committed adultery, he was submitting to Satan's dominion in the area of sexual immorality. Parents are created by God to be a covering of protection for their children. If a parent submits to the devil in a certain area, they lift their spiritual covering from the kids in that area and submit their children to the enemy's devastation and attacks.

This is also why pornography is so common among children and teenagers today. Once a parent gets involved with pornography, whether through movies, internet, or magazines, even if it is just occasionally, the enemy has free reign to show this to the children and get them addicted unless the kids have another spiritual or prayer covering from someone else. We have personally seen in counseling people and heard through other marriage counselors that affairs often stem back to pornography addictions that started in a person's youth.

The exception to this, as we mentioned earlier, is that children remain protected when they are under someone else's spiritual covering. For example, if the other spouse is keeping him or herself sexually pure and prays for the children, God is able to honor this, which is shown by 1 Corinthians 7:14.

For the unbelieving husband is sanctified by the wife, and the unbelieving wife is sanctified by

her husband; otherwise your children would be unclean, but now they are holy.

TRUTH #6...KNOW THE COST OF SIN TO OTHERS

There are people you and I are divinely destined to reach and influence for good. These people are affected by whether or not we choose to stay on course with God. There are things God created you and me to do that no one else can do like we can.

We were once reminded of this truth, how impacting one life is, when we were at the anniversary celebration of the church Dr. Jerry and Carolyn Savelle founded. A man who is a close assistant to Dr. Savelle got up and shared his appreciation of him. He went on to say that even though he had a bad past, his life has been forever changed for good because of God reaching Him through Dr. Savelle's ministry. He thanked Dr. Savelle for living a life of integrity and then, as tears began to flow down his cheeks, he said, "I just want to say thank you for asking Jesus into your heart 36 years ago, because if you hadn't, I don't even want to think about where I would be right now." This is just one example of the impact of a life lived for God.

Future generations will be impacted either positively or negatively based on the choices you and I make today. Sin isn't a private thing. Numbers 32:23 tells us, *"Be sure your sin will find you out."* Psalm 69:5 also says, *"O God, You know my foolishness; and my sins are not hidden from You."* King David who wrote this Psalm knew this better than anybody. When he had committed adultery, the Lord sent a prophet to rebuke and correct him. King David repented and turned away from sin and followed God for the rest of his life.

TRUTH #7...KNOW THE COST OF SIN PERSONALLY

With her enticing speech she caused him to yield, with her flattering lips she seduced him. Immediately, he went after her, as an ox goes to the slaughter...he did not know it would cost his life" (Proverbs 7:21-22).

Friend, if there were only one thing we could get across in this chapter, we would want it to be that sexual immorality costs a very big price, particularly for those who continue in the immoral relationship, leaving their spouse and children and walking away from God because of it. According to this Proverb, it says it will cost a person their life. The word translated as "life" comes from a Hebrew word, that also signifies a person's "vitality" (Strong's #5315). Vitality refers to a person's capacity to live or their mental and physical vigor.

Have you ever heard someone refer to a certain person as being "dead while they are alive." Losing vitality is really the initial stage of losing life completely because a person is dead while they live. They have no vigor for life. They have lost their intensity to live and become more like a robot than a person. This is what happens when someone comes under the influence of Satan and walks away from everything.

We know some wonderful Christian teenagers from a divorced home whose father left the family for another woman and married her. The teenagers have shared how strange it is to go and see their father who once was a loving dad who corrected them when they needed correction, encouraged them in their school activities, and had a personality of his own. Now when they go to visit, they say he is basically like a robot. Things he once liked or disliked, he now has no opinion on. Anything goes, and it is as though he is under a lifeless trance.

This loss of vitality is just the beginning. Revelation 2:21-22 tells us even more,

And I gave her time to repent of her sexual immorality, and she did not repent. Indeed I will cast her into a sickbed, and those who commit adultery with her into great tribulation, unless they repent of their deeds.

Although this is a very serious admonition, great joy and comfort can be found by anyone who leaves sexual sin and chooses not to go back to it, whether they have been in the sin five minutes or fifty years. God never asks a person to clean up their life before they come to Him. He wants us to come to Him first; then He will clean us through Jesus. 2 Peter 3:9 tells us that God *"...is longsuffering toward us, not willing that any should perish but that all should come to repentance."*

It doesn't matter to God how bad a person's sins may be. He loves us all unconditionally no matter what we have done; murderers, sexually immoral, liars, deceivers, you name it. He is waiting to accept us into His family, no matter what we have done. He wants to completely erase our past and give us all a good inheritance through Jesus Christ if we will only let Him! Even if someone has walked away from their relationship with Christ, God is willing to take them back with open arms.

Notice in the last Scripture above, Jesus says He gives a person time to repent. Then, even if someone has refused and experienced tribulation because of submitting to Satan's leadership, He still says *again* at the end, *"unless they repent."* Through this He is reiterating that He doesn't give up on drawing someone to repentance. Anyone who is still breathing can repent, ask Jesus to be their Lord, and receive His help! But remember, there are many people in hell right now who thought they would repent and ask Jesus into their heart before they died, but their death came too suddenly and they never got the chance because they waited too long. Seize the moment and choose to live for Him now!

TRUTH #8...AMY:
KNOW HOW TEMPTATIONS ARISE AND
AVOID THEM

So what should a person be watching for and guarding themselves from? According to Proverbs 7:21–22, a big trap we should guard ourselves from is enticing and flattering speech. This often comes in the form of flirtation, regular compliments or admiration from someone. When a woman pursues a man, enticing speech often takes the form of speaking admiration towards the man's abilities or appearance. It is important to note here that men are more vulnerable to fall into this trap at certain times than others. The following verse gives indication of this:

Do not let your heart turn aside to her ways, do not stray into her paths; for she has cast down many wounded, and all who were slain by her were strong men (Proverbs 7:25-26).

Notice it says that the formerly strong men who get involved in adultery were wounded. I used to read over this verse and not think anything of it, until one day it got my attention. I wondered, "In what way were these men wounded?" Wounded has two definitions. It can either mean a physical wound, or it can mean a hurt to a person's feelings or reputation. We can safely assume this is not referring to the first definition of a wound to the physical body, or the men wouldn't be out and about, getting into an affair. This Scripture is referring to formerly strong men who received a hurt to their feelings or reputation.

A man is created by God to thrive on respect from his wife. However, if the wife is not giving her husband the verbal respect that she should, and the husband is going through challenges such as difficulty at work, loss of a job, financial hardship, or even his wife being downright disrespectful, these are all things that can seriously wound a man emotionally. If he is not going to God to get comfort and healing through these times, he becomes easier prey for the devil to send someone in to try to throw him off course.

We read a marriage article years ago in which a man shared how he lost his job and had come home to tell his wife the news. She said some things to encourage him, which were all very nice to hear. However, what helped him the most was when his wife had sexual intimacy with him. He said this helped build his confidence back up to know that everything would by okay and he would make it through this time. He commented that when a male goes through difficulties, which leave him feeling devalued, a wife's tangible love is the best way she can express her belief in him. Satan also knows this, so when a wife is disrespectful of her husband at these times and the husband does not have a quality relationship with the Lord, Satan often tries to send flirtatious and admiring females in an attempt to go in for the kill.

We have seen that when a female is being pursued, enticing speech is often a man's giving compliments or saying, "I'm here to listen." When a female feels she needs someone to talk to and her husband doesn't seem to have a listening ear, many females will innocently go to a man who shows he will pay attention. This is always a trap of the devil. We have yet to see any situation where it wasn't. We even know of a Christian man and woman who did a Bible study together at work during lunch each day that eventually turned into an affair.

Various studies show that women speak almost twice as many words per day as men. Therefore, it is wise for a husband to give his wife daily communication time. However, even if a man doesn't give his wife quality time, it is never justification for an affair. We can all go to God for help with any need or temptation and He will be faithful to minister His peace to us.

Another way temptations arise is through premarital sexual relations that were never repented of, as well as communicating with old "flames." God does not tell people to avoid premarital sex to hurt them or to try to take away their fun. He does this because He knows that sex outside of the marriage commitment brings bondage rather than bonding. It is a "forbidden fruit" kind of sin because it is done outside of God's blessing.

A couple or person who has engaged in this is wise to repent of the sin, ask God to forgive them, and command in the name of Jesus that all ungodly soul ties and emotional ties be broken off from those past experiences (we can pray this for our spouse as well). Then when any temptation tries to arise, whether it is toward an old boyfriend or girlfriend, or anyone else, a person can take up their shield of faith that Ephesians 6 tells us about and quench that dart of the enemy.

We can stand strong against the temptation and say, "No, I don't desire sin. My body is the temple of the Holy Spirit who dwells in me. I love God and He loves me! Thank you, God, for my spouse and family that You have given me. Thank you that the law of the Spirit of life in Christ Jesus has made me free from the law of sin and death and, therefore, I have victory over sin!"

TRUTH #9...AMY:
ARM YOURSELF WITH THE MIND OF CHRIST

Therefore, since Christ has suffered for us in the flesh, arm yourselves also with the same mind, for he who has suffered in the flesh has ceased from sin (1 Peter 4:1).

As we were preparing to teach the sexual purity portion of one of our marriage conferences one day, 1 Peter 4:1 specifically came to mind. I looked it up and was in awe at how profound this Scripture is. It made complete sense. We have heard the spouse of someone who has been in an affair say things like, "The one thing I could never do is have an affair, because I know how painful it is to be on the suffering side of it now."

In a similar yet much greater way, Christ physically endured the pain of all the sin people in the world would ever commit, so that we would be forgiven of it when we came to God through Jesus. There is no way that Jesus, after suffering all the pain of the cross for our sins, would have risen from the dead, then gone and committed a sin. He knew the price He had paid. His physical body experienced the awful consequences of sin worse than anyone. Through His sufferings, He knew first hand that sin strips people of everything good that God intends them to have.

When counseling people who want help with over-coming temptations, we recommend that when a tempting thought tries to show up, think about Jesus on the cross for you. Think about Him bearing all of the pain and shame for you. When you do this, you won't want to even entertain the thought of sin because we see through the cross how deeply God loves us. Also, if you are married or have children, picture your spouse and your kids. Think about how much you love them and would never want to make them suffer.

When someone experiences temptation or is in sin, they will greatly benefit by thinking daily about how Jesus suffered and paid the price for that specific sin so they could walk free from bondage to it. When we arm ourselves by thinking about how Jesus suffered in His flesh because of any specific sin, we will find it much easier to stay away from the sin.

FINISH YOUR COURSE STRONG

Ecclesiastes 7:8 tells us, *"The end of a thing is better than its beginning; the patient in spirit is better than the proud in spirit."* Jesus has already made the way for believers to live in victory over sin. He desires for us to live a life of freedom through what He gave us as our inheritance.

He left us His Word to be our guide and the Holy Spirit to be our counselor. He made a way for us to not only start strong but also to finish strong! He tells us in His Word that the end (how we finish) is even better than how we start. Some people may be slow starters or may even have walked into some of the devil's traps along the road, but the most important thing is to get on track with God and finish your course strong.

Jesus created a new law, the law of the Spirit of life in Christ Jesus, to override the law of sin and death. When you operate in the law of the Spirit of life, you will be victorious over temptation. Just as John praised the believers he was writing to, saying *"I write to you young men, because you have overcome the wicked one"* (1 John 2:13), we believe the same thing will be said about you one day when you finish your course—that you overcame the wicked one and you also finished your course strong!

How To Overcome Sexual Temptations

1. Know that God has made a way to resist temptations.
2. Daily keep the Word before your eyes and have fellowship with God.
3. Don't allow sin or temptations into your eyes or ears.
4. Shun the appearance of evil.
5. Have trustworthy accountability people (including your spouse).
6. Think about the cost of sin to your children, yourself, your spouse, and others.

Chapter 12

Sexual Intimacy

Behold, you are fair, my love! Behold, you are
fair! You have dove's eyes.
Behold, you are handsome, my beloved! Yes,
pleasant! Also our bed is green
(Song of Solomon 1:15-16).

"According to a large-scale national study, married people have both more and better sex than do their unmarried counterparts. Not only do they have sex more often but they enjoy it more, both physically and emotionally."[5] This statistic should not be surprising, considering that God created sex for the marriage relationship. He made it to be a beautiful union that would not only bring about children to replenish the earth, but also to be an avenue of consummating love, giving of oneself, and bringing enjoyment to the marriage relationship. Since the marriage relationship is metaphorical to our relationship with God, the physical union between husband and wife is also symbolic to the intimacy God desires spiritually with His children. Sex in marriage is intended to be a wonderful blessing from God.

Notice in Song of Solomon 1:15-16, after the married couple voices admiration for each other, the wife states, *"Also our bed is green."* The word green here comes from the Hebrew word that also means to be prosperous and flourishing (Strong's # 7488). When something is prosperous, it is successful and in a thriving condition. To flourish means to be in a state of activity. This gives a picture of how God desires sexual intimacy to be within marriage.

He planned sexual relations within a marriage to prosper, flourish, thrive, and have a regular state of activity. As one writer stated, "It must be part of loving the other for what one is in himself and for what their union means in its exclusiveness and permanence. It is a creative relationship through which a couple expresses the whole meaning and quality of their marriage."[6] God created the physical aspect of a couple's marriage relationship to be a vital and wonderful part of their marital well-being just as He did their spiritual and emotional connection.

Is it this way for everyone? Not always. So whether your physical relationship is as fulfilling as God intended it to be or leaves much to be desired, let us look at how we can benefit from some of the things the Word has to say about sex in marriage.

INTIMACY FROM A MALE PERSPECTIVE

And Rebekah lifted her eyes, and when she saw Isaac she dismounted from her camel . . . Then Isaac brought her into his mother Sarah's tent; and he took Rebekah and she became his wife, and he loved her. So Isaac was comforted after his mother's death (Genesis 24:64, 67).

A male's outlook and perspective on sexual relations with his wife is different than a female's. Women typically do not desire or want sexual intimacy unless they feel loved. A male, on the other hand, often desires sexual intimacy in marriage *in order* to feel loved. Another way of saying this is, a woman's emotions often influence her physical desires. However, a man's physical needs being met often influence his emotions. This is vital for a wife to understand, so that she can be aware of how she can show love to her husband as well as be a minister of God's love to her husband.[7]

Rebekah and Isaac are a classic story of how much sexual intimacy means to a man and how giving a wife can be in this specific area. Notice this was Isaac's first time meeting his wife because of it being an arranged marriage. If we were to read the chapter up to this point we would see how God had specifically chosen Rebekah to be Isaac's wife. When she was brought to him and their marriage was consummated through sexual relations, it says that Isaac loved her.

She freely and willingly gave of herself, making him feel very loved, even though she had not established an emotional relationship with him yet. In turn, we see this caused him to feel love for her. It even tells us that this act of love brought comfort to him regarding the death of his mother. Sexual intimacy is more powerful and God-ordained in marriage than many people even comprehend. If we had any idea the power and strength this brings to a marriage union when done in a spirit of love, couples would make this one of their top priorities in marriage.

Often women are surprised at how their husband can desire intimacy with them even if they have been gone for a week and just returned home. A man can go straight to the bedroom, while a woman wants time to get reacquainted again through visiting or time together. At times, wives have considered a husband who desires sexual relations without a "lead in" to be insensitive and unemotional. However, it is just the contrary. When a man who has missed his wife greatly and knows that sexual intimacy is the way he feels loved, he often just assumes that this will make his wife feel loved also.

Another important detail we find in Scripture is that although men are typically willing to pursue their wife sexually, most men enjoy knowing their wife desires them and like having her be the one who initiates intimacy also. We find the wife as pursuer of her husband in Song of Solomon. It tells us,

By night I sought the one I love; I sought him, but I did not find him. 'I will rise now,' I said… 'I will seek the one I love'…I found the one I love. I held him and would not let him go, until I had brought him to the house of my mother, and into the chamber of her who conceived me (Song of Solomon 3:1-4).

This woman sounds like she is in pursuit of her husband, whom she passionately considers to be her lover also.

For men, sexual intimacy is a way for their wife to show she respects and values them. We have a friend who has a gift of prophecy as mentioned in Romans 12:6, and 1 Corinthians 14:4. He once told us that he was praying for a couple after a church service, and he had a clear vision of a bed with a piece of duct tape all the way down the center of it. He said to the couple, "I see a bed with a piece of duct tape down the center of it. Does this mean anything to you?" They both looked very surprised at him, and the wife said "Yes, I put a piece of duct tape down the center of our bed and told him he can't come on my side anymore." Our pastor friend prayed for some needed things in their marriage, and the woman said she would remove the tape when she got home. This husband probably didn't feel too loved or respected by his wife's cutting him off sexually and even from physical closeness.

This may be an extreme example of a wife being sexually cold toward her husband, but the moral of the story is just the same whether duct tape or being non-responsive to a husband's advances. A man feels loved and valued through sexual intimacy and also has a need to express his love toward his wife in this way. A wise woman will pray "God, I may not be in the mood for this, but I'm asking you to help me become willing right now. I love my husband and therefore, I desire to selflessly give myself to him." As 1 Corinthians 7:4 shares,

The wife does not have authority over her own body, but the husband does. And likewise the husband does not have authority over his own body, but the wife does. Do not deprive one another except with consent for a time, that you may give yourselves to fasting and prayer; and come together again so that Satan does not tempt you because of your lack of self-control.

When believing women look to all of the wonderful examples in the Bible of wives who freely gave of themselves and were joyous lovers to their husbands, God's heart will be seen for sexual intimacy within marriage still today.

AMY: INTIMACY FROM A FEMALE PERSPECTIVE

I am my beloved's, and his desire is toward me (Song of Solomon 7:10).

Sexual intimacy from a female perspective is completely different than a male perspective. As we shared earlier, a woman's emotions often influence her sexual desire. The above Scripture perfectly represents a typical woman's heart. If her husband's words and actions make her feel attractive, loved, and appreciated, she then feels desired by him, and her attitude is much more likely to be one of, "I am my beloved's," and she is willing to show it physically.

The Shulamite and King Solomon, her husband, are a wonderful example of how couples in a marriage are to be continuously admiring of one another. In the book Song of Solomon, Solomon verbally admires or compliments his wife over forty times. The wife also voices admiration of her husband at least thirty times. Obviously, this was a lifestyle in their marriage.

Giving compliments is not something that typically comes naturally for most men. Rather, it usually first comes as an intentional effort to speak blessing over one's spouse because it is the right and loving thing to do. Then, the more we practice, it becomes a part of our nature to be complimentary.

I remember in the early years of our marriage how Shaun would study people who were complimentary and freely offered their praise of others. He would read books about focusing on the best in others. He went from rarely giving compliments to being someone who freely expressed verbal appreciation and compliments in our home. I never even said that I would like him to do this. The more he read the Word he realized that true love builds others up verbally, so he made the choice to teach himself to be complimentary and edifying toward others. As Proverbs 16:23 says, *"The heart of the wise teaches his mouth, and adds learning to his lips."*

Once when Shaun was ministering to a man about the importance of giving compliments to his soon-to-be wife, he recommended the man just start out by making a list of five to ten things that he loved about her, then sitting down and reading the list to her. This man was rather quiet and raised in a home with a father who was not a good role model, so making this list was a big step for him. Several days later, he let Shaun know that he had done what he asked him to do. What was the response? His bride-to-be started to cry and said "Why would you say such nice things about me? I don't deserve that."

This response just goes to show how most females need to know that they are someone special to their husband on a consistent basis. This absolutely beautiful young woman had grown up with a poor image of herself, and for probably the first time, someone let her know she was valuable. A husband who gets a revelation of the importance of complimenting his wife on a regular basis will do his wife as well as his marriage and intimate life a world of good! When a wife feels loved and desired, she is much more likely to have a positive response toward her husband.

The dialogue between the Shulamite and her husband also shows that women like romance. As a couple, you can think of ideas you each feel would build an atmosphere of love and intimacy in your home, which will then improve the romance in your relationship. We know couples who have done this by going out and buying the wife all new sleepwear just to make her feel more attractive. If a wife does not feel pretty, it is often more challenging for her to be intimate because of being self-conscious of her appearance. A husband who has not been having his needs adequately met is wise to focus on building her up with genuine compliments, rather than telling her how inadequate she is.

SHAUN AND AMY: A GIVING HEART

At the same time of discussing the importance of husbands and wives complimenting and edifying each other, we also want to mention that sometimes we see husbands and wives who are waiting for the other one to make them feel loved first. God didn't intend marriage to work like this, thinking of our own needs before our spouse. As a believer in marriage, we should always be willing to give selflessly. Even if a husband has not met the needs of his wife and she doesn't feel loved, a wife can look to God to help her become willing to joyously give of herself just to be a minister of God's love to her husband and vice versa.

We once heard a man say many years ago that he went to the Lord and said, "I don't feel like my wife loves me." He said the Lord responded to his heart by saying, "You should only be focused on loving her, not on whether or not she is loving you. That is between her and Me. You just stay focused on your part of the marriage and trust the rest to Me."

A woman we once worked with is an excellent illustration of this principle. Isabel, a strong and tenacious woman who refused to let go of God's promises, experienced first hand the power of loving her husband unconditionally. Although she and her husband, Tony, now minister to other marriages, things weren't always good. Isabel shared with us how Tony, who had started off on the right foot with God, got sidetracked and stopped reading the Word, started hanging out at the bars with friends, and eventually stopped going to church. She said he became very angry and acted as though she and their children were an obstacle to his having fun. Major fights became a regular thing, and she asked him to go to marital counseling with her. He agreed.

She told us that they visited many marriage counselors, Christian and non-Christian. They were eventually told by almost every one of them who tried to help that their marriage had no hope of being saved. Some counselors even told them, "I don't think God could even save your marriage!" Obviously, those who said this had no idea how powerful our God is! The Word reminds us that *nothing* is impossible for Him (see Luke 1:37). Matthew 19:26 also reminds us, *"With men this is impossible, but with God all things are possible."*

After being given numerous hopeless reports, Isabel turned completely to God and His Word. She studied it and prayed. She boldly declared in her private prayer time that God had given her that husband and Satan would not steal him from their family! She verbally declared that the power of darkness on his life was broken and that he would return to God stronger than ever! Then she asked God to show her how to be the wife He wanted her to be. She asked God to supernaturally give her His ability to love him even when he acted rude and cold. When she prayed these prayers, she had no idea of what was about to happen.

Each day she would ask God what she was supposed to do. Many days he would tell her to make him a nice supper for when he got home. When he would arrive she would be kind and loving. Then when he would say he was going out to the bars and clubs with his friends, she would say, "Let me iron your shirt for you." She would tell him how good he looked and pursue him sexually and be intimate with him. By the time he was finally ready to go he would usually have a change of heart and say, "I guess I'll stay home with you and the kids tonight."

After some time, he still had not returned to the Lord yet, and he told her that he wanted to end the relationship. Knowing that the Word says if the unbeliever wants to depart, let them depart (and he was definitely playing the role of the unbeliever), she said okay. She knew she was supposed to further her education, so she packed up the kids with some of their belongings and drove them to the place where she planned to enroll in college. She told her husband where she was going and let him know that if he didn't want to be married to her anymore that was his choice but she was willing to work things out if he changed his mind and decided to get his life right with God. She put it in God's hands and told God she had done everything she knew that He had asked her to do to love him, and she would live for God no matter what the outcome.

Several months later, her husband contacted her to say he had asked Jesus back into his life and wanted to come live with her and the kids if she would still take him back. Everything worked out beautifully and they now have an awesome testimony of how God's love, shown through a spouse, can heal a hopeless looking marriage.

HOW TO OVERCOME OBSTACLES

Catch us the foxes, the little foxes that spoil the vines, for our vines have tender grapes (Song of Solomon 2:15).

This verse is placed right in the middle of two other verses that talk about this couple's passion and admiration for one another. This seems an odd place to put this, but it was obviously placed there to show us something. What are the little foxes? The interpretation of the original Hebrew word for foxes indicates that this animal was "a burrower" (Strong's #7776). When something burrows, it gets under the surface and digs a hole. This kind of hole is subtly destructive. In fact it often goes unnoticed for some time.

The verse above goes on to say that these foxes or "burrowers" need to be caught; otherwise they will spoil the vines (which also means garden). The word interpreted as *spoil* also means to bind, pervert, destroy, corrupt, offend, or withhold (Strong's #2254).

So what is the writer getting at with this statement placed between two verses about a couple's physical passion and romantic love for each other? He is saying that in a marriage, couples must make a conscious point to catch or eliminate the things that would try to subtly sneak in and destroy or pervert a couple's romantic love and physical relationship together. Anything that would subtly try to bring in offense between the married couple or corrupt their feelings toward each other and anything that would subtly try to come in and cause them to start withholding physical love from one another, needs to be dealt with so that it can no longer burrow to destroy "the fruit in their garden of love," metaphorically speaking.

SHAUN: QUALITY TIME TOGETHER

What are some of the most common "foxes" that try to destroy a couple's romantic love? One "fox" we have seen is when a wife works a full schedule and is also responsible for all the household duties and children, as well as a husband who puts in overtime, then spends much time away in the evening with other activities. A wife can be so exhausted or a husband so busy that the couple develops more of a roommate relationship than a romance relationship. If either of these is a reason for a couple not getting quality time together, we would encourage several things that may help.

First, if this has been an area of confrontation or distress, the wife should not assume that her husband is being insensitive and should just know how to fix this (and vice versa). Second, it is wise to sit down and discuss possible resolutions to the problem. It is to the husband and wife's advantage that needs be met within marriage on a consistent basis in order to maintain a joyful relationship with loving thoughts toward each other, rather than thinking of each other as a roommate or a burden. What distractions can we eliminate from our life that will give us more time to focus on loving each other?

Together compile a list of every idea that may somehow help the situation. Make quality time together a goal and work to achieve this goal as a team. Ideas might include sharing more of the household responsibilities, hiring a housekeeper to clean and do laundry once a week, purchasing prepared meals from a quality store, and having a baby sitter for a weekly date. Ideas may even include a job change or cutback in hours to make more time for each other.

I remember a time when Amy was working a demanding, full-time job, and I also had an extremely full schedule. Amy would come home tired and then make a meal and try to keep up with laundry and housework as well. I would help her with these things as much as I could, but it wasn't enough. After a while, I started to notice she didn't have that same gleam of happiness in her eyes. Her eyes just showed that she needed more sleep!

One day we realized this was one of those "little foxes," so we sat down and talked about how to lighten her load. Together we decided that it would be best for her to cut out several extra obligations she had on some evenings, and we decided on several extra things I would help with around the house. Ultimately, we knew that the best thing was for her to cut back to a part-time job because Amy is someone who feels a need to make homemade meals most of the time and keep the house very orderly. We made a plan, and within six months she was able to cut back, which helped our relationship greatly.

SHAUN AND AMY: CHILDREN AND OUR MARRIAGE

Another "fox" that has been voiced to us by husbands is when the children and the children's activities take regular precedence over romantic interest for the husband. Women typically have an inborn desire to nurture and take care of children; however, when children's needs are continually put before the husband's, it can be damaging to the marriage relationship. There are certainly times when the needs of a child have to come first in a family's time schedule, such as a baby or toddler needing to be fed, and most husbands we have met are very understanding of these things. We are referring here to wives that purposely or maybe subconsciously use busyness with their children as a reason to avoid sexual intimacy.

Children eventually grow up and move out, but our relationship with our spouse is a constant. It is wise to do our very best to maintain a quality relationship, not only in commitment and companionship but also in romance, so when the kids eventually move out, there is still joyous love in the marriage.

Also, maintaining romantic love builds a foundation for our children to learn what a healthy marriage looks like. When we show our kids a good example of the various facets of love, such as dating, holding hands, and being affectionate, we are setting them up to be successful in their own marriage one day. They watch us more closely than we realize.

When our kids are playing, we often sit next to each other talking. When our oldest daughter was two or three, she would stop and watch us from time to time. She loved to see us next to each other and would even say, "Mommy, kiss Daddy!" Then a few minutes later she would say, "Daddy, hug Mommy!" Kids grow to love this because it makes a child feel secure when he or she sees their parents together and being affectionate with each other.

We do our children a huge disservice if we don't make an effort to have a successful marriage in every area. We are their marriage training ground. A few pre-marital classes aren't going to have anywhere near the impact on our children's future marriage as will eighteen years in a home where parents set a positive example on a daily basis.

INCREASING DESIRE

Another "fox" is lack of desire to meet our spouse's physical needs or a lack of interest in our spouse. If a wife or husband struggles with either of these areas, there are several things that can help. Studying and meditating on the Word in the area of sex in marriage will renew a person's mind to the blessing God intended this to be. As Romans 12:2 states,

…Be transformed by the renewing of your mind, that you may prove what is that good and acceptable and perfect will of God.

When a couple focuses on building their marriage overall, just as they did in their early years, they will find the positive feelings return. When honor, value, and quality time together are focused on as we discussed in previous chapters, emotions typically line up with our efforts.

Most people know the classic Disney movie *Beauty and the Beast*. This story line actually holds much truth for both males and females. The Beast, who is very ugly, loves Belle, the beauty. He eventually wins her love in return by being kind, considerate, and loving toward her. This is often the case in life as well. Even if someone who is less than attractive treats the one they are interested in right, the feelings often become reciprocated. The truth of the matter is, people are often more attracted to a person based on how valued they make them feel than by their looks. Looks are often what initially attract a person, but enthusiasm, kindness, and a considerate personality are what help a relationship last over the long run.

PREVIOUS RELATIONSHIPS

Another "fox" can be past hurts from previous relationships that try to affect the romantic life adversely. If a spouse has been sexually abused in their past and has never recovered from it emotionally (which is more often an occurrence with women), often this can be a reason that someone avoids sexual intimacy. A woman who has been abused and never emotionally healed will sometimes find every excuse under the sun not to be intimate with her husband until she allows God to minister healing to her.

If this is the case, the wife and husband should seek help. They should pray together over this issue, asking God to heal the wife's heart and emotions, as well as pray healing Scriptures over her. Get counsel from a trusted and respected Christian counselor who has helped others recover and become happy in their marriage. As we mentioned earlier, Jesus told us in Matthew 19:26, *"...With God all things are possible."*

Past sexual relationships outside of marriage also cause a person to have emotional baggage that God never intended in a marriage. It is wise to pray for yourself and your spouse if there were any past relationships. As you pray, command that all soul ties from previous relationships be broken off from yourself and your spouse in the name of Jesus. Pray that both of you will never think of people from your past in any way other than you would think of a sister or a brother. Also, make the choice to get rid of things you still have from those people. Jewelry, gifts, pictures and things of this nature from past relationships have no place in a person's life when they love and are committed to someone else in marriage.

OTHER LITTLE FOXES

Another "fox" may be negative comments made to a person that lodged in their heart and created feelings of fear or inadequacy. We have had women married many years tell us that they have always struggled with this area because of things like their mother or an aunt making comments when they were young such as, "Sex is something you have to do to please your husband, but you will never enjoy it." The truth is, *"Marriage is honorable among all, and the bed undefiled"* (Hebrews 13:4). This is saying that sex within marriage is pure. Anything God created, when it is used in the way He created it to be used, is good.

Another "fox" is the deception of pornography. Many men and women use pornography and masturbation, which is most often an addiction that started as a teen or young adult. Although it may seem harmless to many people, this is actually very destructive to married and unmarried people alike.

Dr. Doug Weiss, a highly successful and respected counselor of over 20 years who specializes in helping people get free from sex addictions, says that when a man or woman has sex addictions, it stops them from reaching their full potential of who God created them to be. He has stated that when a man gets free from a sex addiction, statistics show their income doubles! Pornography and other addictions will hinder so many areas of a person's life and potential. As Dr.

Weiss expressed so perfectly, "Satan wants to seduce people in order to reduce people."[8] When people get hooked, their divine destiny is stolen in so many areas.

We need to remember our body has three owners: God, our spouse, and then ourselves. If we are tempted with sexual sin, we should go to God, our spouse, and even a trusted Christian mentor if necessary. The good news is that there is deliverance from sexual addictions. It doesn't have to rule over people and hinder them all of their lives.

A Christian counselor once told about a woman who came to him for help. She had asked her husband many times if they could start praying together but he always refused for one reason or another. The counselor responded that he has found if a husband refuses to pray with his wife, taking his place as the spiritual head of the home, it is often because he struggles with a sex addiction. God's design of sex was intended to function spirit, soul, and body. A spiritual bond is first created through a couple who prays together, an emotional bond is created through the couple sharing thoughts and activities with each other, and then the sexual intimacy bond is built.

God wants his children to be fulfilled and happy in their marriage. He made every aspect of marriage to be a blessing. He also made a way for all pains from a person's past and all addictions to be healed. When we look to God's Word and stand upon His promises, we will then be able to experience the newness of life He intended for us through Jesus Christ our Lord and Healer.

BLESSED BY GOD

God created the physical area to work in harmony with the spiritual and emotional areas. For a relationship to be truly strong and fulfilling, as God created it to be, it is important to have all three areas in order to experience the blessing God intended a marriage to be. When a couple grows in their spiritual and emotional bond, they will typically see growth in the physical as well. Sometimes, this must be an intentional and concentrated effort of love on the part of one or even both of the spouses.

Any extra effort in this area will pay off in the long run in building a strong and fulfilling marriage that is a gift to both husband and wife. It is to both the husband and wife's benefit to ensure their spouse's sexual and affection needs are being met consistently. God made the physical union to be a wonderful bond in a marriage, and it will be when each spouse places the other first.

Creating A Strong Physical Bond
1. Voice admiration and compliments to your spouse.
2. Wives, remember sex is a way to show love to your husband.

3. Husbands, remember kind actions and loving words are a way to show your wife love.

4. Eliminate "the little foxes" that try to hinder sexual intimacy.

5. Remember God's design of sex is to have all areas in order, spirit, soul, and body.

Chapter 13

A Vision Together

**Write the vision and make it plain on tablets,
that he may run who reads it (Habakkuk 2:2).**

Zig Ziglar once said that when a person has a strong vision and a problem arises, the problem will be like a pebble on the beach they simply kick out of the way. However, if a person has no vision and a problem arises, it will be like a tidal wave washing them into the sea. We have found through working with couples, that this saying is very true. Setbacks and problems are just a pebble on the beach for couples who clearly know their God-given vision together, but for a couple with no clear purpose and plan, problems often seem to become tidal waves. This is most likely why strife in a marriage and lack of a Christ-centered vision often go hand in hand. Without a strong eternal purpose together, believers are often washed into the same tidal wave of marriage disappointment that the world struggles with.

It has been recorded that within the first five years of marriage the number one struggle marriages deal with is financial hardship.[9] Although lack of wisdom with finances and lack of self-control in spending are frequent causes for financial hardship, we strongly believe one of the biggest roots to financial problems within marriage is that many couples do not know their God-given purpose for being together, which often results in a focus on things of the world rather than the things of God.

In our early years of marriage, we had very little. There was not any extra money for dates, gifts, or extra purchases of any sort. We thank God that as we look back on it, we never had one argument over money. We believe a large reason for this was that our vision together was so strong. We refused to get discouraged by the financial situation we were in because we knew God had a plan for our lives together. We also knew Matthew 6:33 says, *"But seek first the kingdom of God and His righteousness, and all these things shall be added to you."* We trusted God that if we pursued His plan for our life and marriage, He would take care of us and we would experience the goodness the Bible talks about.

The Bible encourages us to have a vision and make it plain, so we can run with it. Sometimes couples we encounter have some vision as an individual for their career or maybe parenting, which is good, but more is needed. Unless a couple has a focused, eternal purpose in their relationship together, they often end up just striving after material things as the rest of the world does. However, when a couple has a Christ-centered vision, they are no longer satisfied with the status quo of just going to church on Sundays, reading their Bible on occasion, then living like the rest of the world throughout the week, doing little to nothing of eternal value.

God created us as humans with a desire to do something of lasting value and to be a gift to the lives of others. We were created in God's image, and He does things of eternal value. Therefore we also have an inherent desire to create something meaningful with our lives. Sin has tried its best to corrupt this desire in people, but when a person gives their life to God, the desire for their God-given purpose is renewed in them. Our goal today is to stir up that desire in you if it has been lying dormant or untapped. God has a plan for you to do something to change the world with lasting, eternal impact, not just as an individual but also as a couple.

SHAUN: TAKING DOMINION TOGETHER

What was the first responsibility given to mankind by God? We find it in Genesis 1:26,

Let us make man in Our image, according to Our likeness; let them have dominion over the fish of the sea, over the birds of the air, and over the cattle, over all the earth and over every creeping thing that creeps on the earth.

God gave man the responsibility of having dominion over the earth. He also gave him a helper to assist with taking dominion:

And the Lord God said, 'It is not good that man should be alone; I will make him a helper comparable to him (Genesis 2:18).

Notice the man's helper was made to be comparable to him. "Comparable" typically means to be similar, parallel to, suited to, or matched together. In other words, the husband and wife are made by God to be perfectly suited to each other or "a match made in heaven." A helper is someone who brings aid or assistance with the task at hand. Putting these meanings all together gives us a great picture of how a married couple is created to work. The two go side by side, using their different gifts and abilities to compliment each other and accomplish a unified goal in the area God has called them to take dominion.

In what area has God called you and your spouse to take dominion? Do you know how your gifts and abilities compliment each other to take dominion for God's kingdom? We remember our early days when we were just learning about this. We knew I was called to ministry. I was thankful that Amy always saw herself as part of the ministry. She always treated ministry as our goal, rather than my goal, and I welcomed this.

Amy has many talents that, at times, have seemed to have nothing to do with ministry. For example, she is a gifted makeup artist and worked in the early years of our marriage as a modeling instructor and makeup artist for a well-known modeling school and agency. We both believed it was right for her to take this job and she excelled greatly in it, achieving the company's highest award as an instructor. We never dreamed this would fit into ministry one day, but God knew otherwise. Years later, she became a makeup artist for several well-known television ministries.

The longer we are married, the more we see how God has perfectly planned our different gifts and abilities to compliment and benefit each other. Our vision started out very basic, but has continued to grow as we have sought God for direction in our calling together. I also remember how Amy would regularly help me when I was finishing college. She would often invest her evenings helping me study. She did other things to help me with college as well. Noticing that I was very reward motivated, she would go shopping every semester to buy gifts for me, wrap them individually and put them in a basket. She had an "A" basket and a "B" basket for when I had tests. The A gifts were better than the B gifts so, based on the grade I earned, I got a gift from the appropriate box. In two years I went from having a low B average to graduating with honors. Her help greatly improved my performance in achieving our goal of ministry education.

SHAUN AND AMY: A UNIFIED, CHRIST-CENTERED VISION

Most of us have met people who claim to be a self-made man or woman. They like to think they are not dependent on anyone, including God. The problem with this mindset is that God did not make people to function independent of one another. We read in Ephesians 4:14-16 about this,

...That we should no longer be children, tossed to and fro and carried about by every wind of doctrine, by the trickery of men, in the cunning craftiness of deceitful plotting, but, speaking the truth in love, may grow up in all things into Him who is the head—Christ—from whom the whole body, joined and knit together by what every joint supplies, according to the effective working by which every part does its share, causes growth of the body for the edifying of itself in love.

According to this, we see each person plays a part in fulfilling a need to be met in the whole unified body of Christ. As a marriage team, we are also equipped to supply a certain part (our area of dominion) to the body of Christ as a whole. The gifts we have work directly together with our spouse's gifts to cause growth in the church body as well as in the body of our own household to edify each other in love.

We will use an example for this of a couple we know. They are a great illustration of how a couple who is not in full-time ministry can utilize a regular calling to create eternal vision and value. This couple has many gifts that fit together wonderfully, but we will focus on how the husband's God-given ability in business works together with one of his wife's God-given gifts to create eternal value. The husband is a very successful businessman and the wife has chosen to be a stay-at-home mother. The husband is gifted in leadership and finances, and the wife has the gift of giving, as talked about in Romans 12:6 and 8,

> **Having then gifts differing according to the grace that is given to us, let us use them...he who gives, with liberality...**

The wife, like few people we have ever seen before, has a gift of knowing when someone needs money and knowing when they are supposed to sow (give) something into someone's life. The husband is very good at saving for their future, including college money for their children, retirement, and things of that nature, yet most importantly he is very open to being an avenue for God to work through whenever God asks them to give. They both understand that although earthly investments are important, the greatest investment someone can make is investing in God's kingdom, where moth and rust do not destroy (see Matthew 6:19).

The wife of this couple has come to us before and said, "You know that young single mom you introduced me to at such and such a place last year, can I get her address from you? She's been on my heart with Christmas coming up." Another time she called and said, "Remember that one single woman you used to work with last year? She's been on my heart lately and I feel like we are supposed to send her something. Can you find out her address?" In each of these cases, it was very timely and very much needed in the people's lives.

In addition to being led by the Holy Spirit from day to day, they focus on consistently giving to certain ministries each month in order to build God's kingdom, which produces long-lasting, eternal value and reward. They have been one of the most consistent givers to our ministry every month for many years without fail. Even when we were still in our preparation stages of college, as well as getting our ministry off the ground, they by faith saw our long-term vision and knew our commitment to its fulfillment. They chose to invest in our ministry vision from God, making it a part of their own ministry vision by becoming financial partners.

This couple is quite a contrast to the story of the man in the Bible who did not have a Christ-centered vision, but rather, only a temporal one. We find it in Luke 12:16-21,

The ground of a certain rich man yielded plen-tifully. And he thought within himself, saying,

'What shall I do, since I have no room to store my crops?' So he said, 'I will do this; I will pull down my barns and build greater, and there I will store all my crops and my goods. And I will say to my soul, "Soul you have many goods laid up for many years; take your ease; eat, drink, and be merry."' But God said to him, 'Fool! This night your soul will be required of you; then whose will those things be which you have provided?' So is he who lays up treasure for himself, and is not rich toward God.

Some people pass over this last sentence, thinking it is condemning people for having earthly investments. It is not. We can see from the life of Joseph in the Old Testament that God encourages saving. The key to this sentence is the phrase, "and is not rich toward God." The only question we need to find an answer for in our checkbook ledger is: "Are we consistently rich toward God, or is our main focus earthly goods and investments?"

GETTING ON THE SAME PAGE

A young ministry student once told me he and his wife had just discussed how they felt it would be more difficult to minister now that they were married. In their minds, they thought of marriage and family as a constraint rather than a blessing from God. When I asked why, he said they would not be able to pick up and leave as easily, and he gave several other reasons that were classic examples of someone who was looking at their own abilities rather than God's multiplication abilities. My response to his statement was, "Yes, you may not be able to leave anytime you want, but when you and your wife learn to work your two sets of God-given abilities together into one unified ministry, you will have more power to minister than you would have otherwise!"

A unified vision for God is vital to being able to utilize our marriage to the greatest degree God planned it to operate. As we looked at the chapter on resolving strife, Satan always looks to get a foothold in marriages in an attempt to divide this powerful union the Lord has created. If bitterness, selfishness, anger, or pride can take root, then Satan has an extremely good chance of stopping a couple from fulfilling the purpose God has for their marriage.

When a couple is married, it is vital to have their vision set clearly before them. They must know what God's purpose and plan is for their specific marriage, which will cause a bond of unity and, we believe, marital permanence between the husband and wife. As Habakkuk 2:2 says, *"...Write the vision and make it plain on tablets, that he may run who reads it."* Many couples run, living life from day to day, but have not stopped to ask God where they are supposed to run or why God gave them that specific partner for their life's course. The good news is, even if a couple has been married many years and never had a Christ-centered vision, it is never too late. God has a vision for us as a couple, no matter what our age.

A young man once told me that he knew what God had called him to do (he believed he was called to a certain area of ministry), but he said his wife had no idea what her purpose was. She would talk to her husband about this, but at the time she could not seem to find the answer. We have found this mindset to be fairly common, especially in younger couples.

If a wife doesn't understand her calling and how it fits with her husband, or vice versa, it is typically because the couple has not sat down together and allowed God to develop a joint vision. Some couples think this isn't necessary. They may think that because they are believers their life will just all come together the way God wants it to without any set plan. But as motivational speaker Zig Ziglar says, "Aim for nothing and you'll hit it every time."

We sometimes see a husband or a wife with a very strong personal vision wondering why their spouse doesn't get on board with them. Wives often are waiting to be invited or encouraged by the husband to be a part of the vision. Both men and women like to hear their spouse say things like, "I don't know how I could do this without your help. You are so important to me!" The more our spouse feels needed and appreciated, the more likely they are to want to be a part of a unified vision.

Often men or women may not come right out and say it, but their actions imply they are only interested in doing their own thing and never make their spouse feel a part of their life and goals. However, when a believing couple discovers the power of a unified vision and how simple it is to apply this to their marriage, amazing and powerful things begin to happen!

We once heard a testimony about the scientist who was the creator of the stationary satellite. Scientists had tried for years to get a satellite to orbit the earth in a stationary rotation, but none could figure out how to do it. This scientist and his wife, both together and separately, would invest time praying in the Spirit over this need. With God's help through answered prayer, he was the scientist who figured out what no one else could. This man took his calling as a scientist and allowed his wife to be part of the vision through having her pray the answer into manifestation with him.

Women have an inborn desire to help others, which is demonstrated by the fact that females predominantly occupy the helping professions such as nursing and teaching. If a wife is not allowed to assist her husband as a teammate in some way and does not feel a purpose with him in a unified calling, she will often develop her own set of goals, which may bring division and frequent separation to the home. Sometimes a wife may even seem to fight against the husband's calling. A wife who does this is often really saying, "Explain to me how you see me fitting in with this vision and encourage me in my part of it, because I don't see your need for me as a teammate right now."

I sometimes sit and think about Amy's gifts and talents and how they fit into our calling together. Then I share with her what I've thought about. At times we haven't always seen how everything would fit together but if we both have peace about something, we proceed forward.

For example, I used to do street witnessing, but Amy could not go with me because of having a young child at home. After I had received direction for this, Amy said several days later that it had been in her heart that she was to be praying for the evangelism team and myself as we went out on Friday nights. We had great miracles happen on those nights and many new commitments to Christ. I would come home and tell Amy about what happened, and she experienced the same joy I had because she took part in the night through prayer.

A VISION WITH VALUE

How do we create a vision together with lasting value? This first begins with understanding what vision really is. When Habakkuk 2:2 says, *"Write the vision and make it plain...,"* the Hebrew word used for *vision* actually means a dream or a revelation that comes from God (Strong's #2377). So creating our vision together first begins with receiving a revelation or dream in our hearts from God. We can pray and ask God what we are called to do with our spouse.

Sometimes people know even as children what they are called to do. God places this in our spirit from the moment we are conceived. The Bible even says, *"Before I formed you in the womb I knew you; before you were born I sanctified you; I ordained you a prophet to the nations"* (Jeremiah 1:5). This means when He created us, He knew all along what our purpose would be. When we ask God to reveal to us His dream and plan for our life together, we can trust that He will be faithful to show us.

Together with our spouse, we can write down each of our gifts and talents and how we believe they are meant to work with our spouse's gifts and calling. As God reveals His plan for us, we then turn that plan into goals. In Philippians 3:14 Paul states, *"I press toward the goal for the prize of the upward call of God in Christ Jesus."* Notice Paul did not say that he pressed toward the prize. He said he pressed toward the *goal*, which is also translated as "mark" in the King James Version.

Paul didn't aimlessly say, "Boy, I sure hope I'll get a prize or reward someday for having done something right while I was on the earth!" No, Paul said he pressed toward a goal. He knew it was a Christ-centered and Christ-directed goal that would please God. God wants each of us in our personal life and marriage to have goals that we plan and attain under His leading, so we can accomplish the purpose for which He placed us on earth. He can also then give us greater eternal rewards when we get to heaven!

When we know what God has called us to do, we can make intermediate goals with action plans as a mark to measure our success in moving toward the ultimate goal. Some questions we might ask ourselves are: Do these goals further God's kingdom? Do our individual goals fit into our ultimate goal as a team in marriage? What do we need to do to prepare ourselves to fulfill each goal? What roadblocks might we need to overcome on the way and how will we overcome them? When do we plan to achieve each goal?

Team goals may encompass areas such as financial goals of consistent giving above the tithe to certain ministries each month, having a daily family Bible study time or prayer time together, volunteering together in a certain area of the church, sponsoring children who live in poverty in another country through a trusted ministry, or doing short term missions work together. It is also important to have goals in other areas as well, such as quality marriage time, family time, financial, exercise, and things of this nature. Just remember to keep God first place.

A REALITY CHECK

We once heard a story about a couple that attended a marriage conference and got a big wake up call. They said the conference speaker mentioned how most Christian couples just want to be financially secure and happy, and then if God is pleased with them, that would be great too. The conference speaker went on to say the trouble with this mindset is that when we make security and happiness our top goals, these things become impossible to attain because we are seeking our own pleasures rather than seeking the kingdom of God first. When this couple analyzed where the majority of their money went and how they spent the majority of their time, they realized they were not seeking the kingdom of God first but, rather, living primarily for personal gain.

The couple wrote out new goals and then began to boldly pursue them. They personally and financially began supporting a marriage ministry, a ministry to feed and train the poor, and several pastors. They determined to work with and support the same pastors, churches, and ministries each month, knowing that a consistent, focused effort will produce more lasting results than sporadic involvement. Years later, this couple commented that after they changed their focus from desiring a big house, financial security, and promotion to instead pursuing the furthering of God's kingdom, all of these former desires had been added to them without their even trying.

This couple is living proof that when we take care of what concerns God, He will take care of what concerns us. God passionately wants to reward you and your family for doing what He has called you to do. He is just looking for avenues through which He can pour out His blessing on you! When we as believers set eternal goals and advance in the steps to His ultimate plan for our lives, this creates wonderful avenues for His goodness to pour out in the greatest measure on our life and the lives of those around us. May you and your spouse passionately pursue and achieve all He has called you to do and may you be rewarded greatly for making an eternal difference in the lives of others!

Vision Together
1. Sit down as a couple and write your vision together.
2. Be sure to include goals for contributing to God's kingdom spirit, soul, and body.
3. Remember that God will make sure your personal goals are met as you keep Him and His priorities in first place.

Conclusion

God Has A Good Plan For You

No matter what has happened in your past, no matter what the future seems to hold, you can make the choice today to apply the simple truth of God's Word to your relationships. It will make all the difference between a dull, boring, possibly even painful life, or a joyful, successful, productive life that has eternal value and reward! Circumstances in life do not have to dictate our attitudes or responses to others. We can daily choose to find something to be thankful for, whether it is healthy children or knowing we have a wonderful eternity in heaven because we have made Jesus our Lord and Savior.

Choose today to treat those in your house as uncommonly special and important people. Let them know everyday that they have great value to you and to God. Whoever we treat as common will become common to us. However, those we treat with value will become more and more valuable to us. Make thankfulness your target every day. Appreciate the little things, and life will become more meaningful to you and those around you. A thankful heart really does become a happy heart.

We encourage you to keep this book nearby and read again certain chapters that stand out to you in the months to come. When we keep marriage and relationship fresh in our mind, we are then able to apply the needed skills to be successful consistently. Your spouse and children are a gift from God to you, to value, cherish, and grow in a relationship with the Lord together.

We believe you will pursue and attain all God has for you and your family. Just remember that love never fails. When you walk in God's love, the course ahead of you will be made clear. We believe in your success because the Successful One (God Himself) is living in you.

Pastors Shaun and Amy

Shaun and Amy Gustafson
P.O. Box 8113
Rochester, MN 55903
www.wolrochester.org

ENDNOTES

1. Copyright 2002 by David Popenoe, the National Marriage Project at Rutgers University, New Brunswick, N.J.

2. *Eerdmans Bible Dictionary*, Copyright 1987 by Wm. B. Eerdmans Publishing Co. p. 49.

3. *Pictorial Bible Dictionary*, Copyright 1963, 1964, Zondervan Publishing House, p. 512.

4. Keys To Loving Relationships, Gary Smalley Seminar, Copyright 1998.

5. Copyright 2002 by David Popenoe, the National Marriage Project at Rutgers University, New Brunswick, N.J.

6. This is not true with a couple before marriage because although they may have sexual desires before marriage, they are to honor God and the woman they are dating or engaged to. If they keep themselves in relationship with God, His grace will be sufficient to get them through this time, abstaining from sex until marriage.

7. Information and quote taken from Dr. Doug Weiss seminar held at Heritage of Faith Christian Center in Crowley, TX, February 2007.
8. Statistical information taken from Church On The Way. Personal interview done with Pastors Mark and Cindy Henderson, May 2002.

OTHER RESOURCES

1. STRONG'S EXHAUSTIVE CONCORDANCE OF THE BIBLE by James Strong, Hendrickson Publishers.

CPSIA information can be obtained
at www.ICGtesting.com
Printed in the USA
BVHW07s2015111018

529783BV00029B/651/P

9 781615 794911